GRADES 3-5

W9-BNR-470

Brain-Compatible ACTIVITIES

David A. Sousa

CORWIN PRESS
Classroom

For information:

Corwin Press
A SAGE Publications Company
2455 Teller Road
Thousand Oaks, California 91320
CorwinPress.com

SAGE Publications, Ltd.
1 Oliver's Yard
55 City Road
London EC1Y 1SP
United Kingdom

SAGE Publications India Pvt. Ltd.
B 1/I 1 Mohan Cooperative
Industrial Area
Mathura Road, New Delhi
India 110 044

SAGE Publications Asia-Pacific Pvt. Ltd.
33 Pekin Street #02-01
Far East Square
Singapore 048763

Printed in the United States of America.

ISBN 978-1-4129-5272-9

This book is printed on acid-free paper.

08 09 10 11 12 10 9 8 7 6 5 4 3 2 1

Executive Editor: Kathleen Hex
Managing Developmental Editor: Christine Hood
Editorial Assistant: Anne O'Dell
Developmental Writer: Jessica Inlow
Proofreader: Bette Darwin
Art Director: Anthony D. Paular
Cover Designer: Lisa Riley
Interior Production Artist: Karine Hovsepian

BRAIN-COMPATIBLE ACTIVITIES

TABLE OF CONTENTS

Connections to Standards

This chart shows the national academic standards that are covered in each chapter.

LANGUAGE ARTS	Standards are covered on pages
Read a wide range of print and nonprint texts to build an understanding of texts, of self, and of the cultures of the United States and the world; to acquire new information; to respond to needs and demands of society and the workplace; and for personal fulfillment (includes fiction and nonfiction, classic, and contemporary works).	22
Adjust the use of spoken, written, and visual language (e.g., conventions, style, vocabulary) to communicate effectively with a variety of audiences and for different purposes.	13
Apply knowledge of language structure, language conventions (e.g., spelling and punctuation), media techniques, figurative language, and genre to create, critique, and discuss print and nonprint texts.	10
Conduct research on issues and interests by generating ideas and questions and by posing problems. Gather, evaluate, and synthesize data from a variety of sources (e.g., print and nonprint texts, artifacts, people) to communicate discoveries in ways that suit the purpose and audience.	22

MATHEMATICS	Standards are covered on pages
Numbers and Operations—Understand numbers, ways of representing numbers, relationships among numbers, and number systems.	39
Algebra—Use mathematical models to represent and understand quantitative relationships.	27
Geometry—Use visualization, spatial reasoning, and geometric modeling to solve problems.	32
Measurement—Understand measurable attributes of objects and the units, systems, and processes of measurement.	35

978-1-4129-5272-9

SOCIAL STUDIES	Standards are covered on pages
Understand individual development and identity.	54
Understand how people organize for the production, distribution, and consumption of goods and services.	57
Understand relationships among science, technology, and society.	48

SCIENCE	Standards are covered on pages
Science as Inquiry—Ability to conduct scientific inquiry.	70
Life Science—Understand characteristics of organisms.	63
Life Science—Understand organisms and environments.	63
Earth and Space Science—Understand changes in the earth and sky	74
Science in Personal and Social Perspectives—Understand populations, resources, and environments.	57

Introduction

Brain-compatible activities are often louder and contain more movement than traditional lessons. Research has shown that purposeful talking and movement encourage retention of new learning. While this may seem out of your comfort zone at first, good classroom management and a willingness to try new things is all that is needed to implement these activities in any classroom. Once you and your students become accustomed to brain-compatible strategies, you will find it difficult to go back to more traditional teaching methods. Students (and teachers!) enjoy lessons that actively involve their brains, and the brains that are actively involved are the brains that learn.

It has been estimated that teachers make over 1,600 decisions per day. As professional educators, it is our job to be familiar with current research to make sure those decisions count for our students. This book is filled with activities that are supported by brain research. These activities will help increase learning because they are structured to maximize the brain's learning potential.

How to Use This Book

The activities in this book are designed using a brain-compatible lesson plan format. There are nine components of the plan, but not all nine are necessary for every lesson. Those components that are most relevant to the learning objective should be emphasized.

- Anticipatory set
- Learning objective
- Purpose
- Input
- Modeling
- Check for understanding
- Guided practice
- Closure
- Independent practice

Each of the components is described in detail in my book titled *How the Brain Learns, Third Edition* (2006). Refer to it for more brain-compatible research and other teaching strategies.

When using the activities in this book, read through the activity first. Then begin the preparations for the lesson. Make sure to follow the lesson plan format to ensure maximum learning potential. However, be flexible enough to meet the needs of all learners in your class. A positive classroom climate is essential for retention.

Put It Into Practice

How the brain learns has been of particular interest to teachers for centuries. Now, in the twenty-first century, there is new hope that our understanding of this remarkable process called teaching and learning will improve dramatically. A major source of that understanding is coming from the sophisticated medical instruments that allow scientists to peer inside the living—and learning—brain.

As we examine the clues that this research yields about learning, we recognize its importance to the teaching profession. Every day teachers enter their classrooms with lesson plans, experience, and the hope that what they are about to present will be understood, remembered, and useful to their students. The extent that this hope is realized depends largely on the knowledge base teachers use in designing those plans and, perhaps more important, in the strategies and techniques they select for instruction. Teachers try to change the human brain every day. The more they know about how it learns, the more successful they will be.

Some of the recent research discoveries about the brain can and should affect teaching and learning. For example, this research has:

- reaffirmed that the human brain continually reorganizes itself on the basis of input. This process, called neuroplasticity, continues throughout our life but is exceptionally rapid in the early years. Thus, the experiences the young brain has in the home and at school help shape the neural circuits that will determine how and what that brain learns in school and later.

- revealed more about how the brain acquires spoken language.

- developed scientifically based computer programs that dramatically help young children with reading problems.

- shown how emotions affect learning, memory, and recall.

- suggested that movement and exercise improve mood, increase brain mass, and enhance cognitive processing.

- tracked the growth and development of the teenage brain to better understand the unpredictability of adolescent behavior.

A much fuller explanation of these discoveries and their implications for school and the classroom can be found in my book, *How the Brain Learns, Third Edition* (2006), published by Corwin Press. This book is designed as a practical classroom resource to accompany that text. The activities in this book translate the research and strategies for brain-compatible teaching and learning into practical, successful classroom activities. They focus on the brain as the organ of thinking and learning, and take the approach that the more teachers know about how the brain learns, the more instructional options they have at hand. Increasing teachers' options during the dynamic process of instruction also increases the likelihood that successful learning will occur.

Some general guidelines provide the framework for these activities:

- Learning engages the entire person (cognitive, affective, and psychomotor domains).

- The human brain seeks patterns in its search for meaning.

- Emotions affect all aspects of learning, retention, and recall.

- Past experience always affects new learning.

- The brain's working memory has limited capacity and processing time.

- Lecture usually results in the lowest degree of retention.

- Rehearsal is essential for retention.

The activities in this book also are backed by research-based rationale for using particular instructional strategies, including cooperative learning groups, differentiated instruction, discussion, movement, manipulatives, metaphors, visualization, and so on, all of which can increase motivation and retention of learned concepts. Those who are familiar with constructivism will recognize many similarities in the ideas presented here. The research is yielding more evidence that knowledge is not only transmitted from the teacher to the learners but is transformed in the learner's mind as a result of cultural and social influences.

The classroom is a laboratory where teaching and learning processes meet and interact. This laboratory is not static but constantly changing as intensive research produces new discoveries about how the brain learns and retains information. The more information educators have, the more they can adjust their understanding and instructional strategies to ensure students are using their brains to the fullest capacity. As we discover more about how the brain learns, we can devise strategies that make the teaching-learning process more efficient, effective, and enjoyable.

CHAPTER 1

Language Arts

The human brain is not hardwired for reading. Our brains can master spoken language quickly. However, because the act of reading is not a survival skill, the brain requires explicit training in reading. Learning to read requires three neural systems and the development of skills that work together to help the brain decode abstract symbols into meaningful language. The visual processing system sees the printed word; the auditory processing system sounds out the word; and the frontal lobe integrates the information to produce meaning. It is a bidirectional and parallel process that requires phonemes to be processed at the same time. Reading is testament to the brain's remarkable ability to sift through input and establish meaningful patterns and systems.

Reading is one of the most difficult skills for the brain to master, and under current legislation, students must master it at an earlier age than ever before. It is crucial, therefore, that you choose activities that capture students' attention and promote retention. While the following activities are content-specific, they can be easily modified to fit your curriculum.

As the brain is developing skills to decode meanings of sounds and symbols, it is creating semantic and syntactic networks that will aid in communication. Verbal and written communication involve syntax and semantics to create meaning. The syntactic network uses the rules of language, or grammar. The semantic network combines the components of language and the mind's search for meaning. The brain holds two separate stores for semantics, one for verbally based information and another for image-based information. Using concrete images to teach abstract concepts will greatly increase retention. The brain builds on speaking skills to develop and refine all language abilities—speaking, reading, writing, and grammar.

> **Scientific research suggests that reading instruction include a balance between the development of phonemic awareness and the use of enriched texts to help learners with syntax and semantics.**

Newspaper Noun Narratives

Standard

Apply knowledge of language structure, language conventions (e.g., spelling and punctuation), media techniques, figurative language, and genre to create, critique, and discuss print and nonprint texts.

Objective

Students will identify nouns in written text and use nouns in narrative writing.

Anticipatory Set

As students enter the classroom or prepare for the lesson, sit in a chair with your legs propped up and read the newspaper. Allow time for student interest to build, and then act like you are surprised to see them: *I bet you are wondering what I'm doing. It just so happens that I am working on a writing project!*

Read all about it!

Purpose

Tell students that authors look to many different places, including newspapers, to find ideas for their writing. Explain that they are going to use a newspaper to find nouns for a narrative writing assignment.

Input

Remind students that nouns are naming words. They name people, places, and things in a sentence. Examples of nouns are animals, books, people, machines, fruit, buildings, or anything that is a person, place, or thing. Invite volunteers to point out some nouns in the classroom.

Modeling

Pair up students with partners. Give each pair a newspaper page and a highlighter. Then show them your newspaper page. Read aloud a paragraph and say: *There are many nouns in this paragraph. I am going to use my highlighter to highlight all the nouns I find.* Model highlighting the nouns for students.

Inform students that they are going to use their nouns to write a narrative. Explain that a narrative is writing that tells a story. Show a transparency of the **Newspaper Narrative reproducible (page 12)** on the overhead. Demonstrate how to write a narrative using five nouns from your highlighted newspaper page. Make your story simple and humorous to keep students interested and focused on the lesson.

Newspaper Narrative Page 12

Check for Understanding

Make sure students understand that there are two steps in the activity. First, they will work in pairs to find and highlight nouns in the newspaper. Then they will choose five of those nouns to write a narrative.

Guided Practice

Invite student pairs to find and highlight nouns on their own newspaper pages. Give students five minutes to find and highlight as many nouns as they can. Then give everyone a copy of the Newspaper Narrative reproducible. Instruct students to choose five nouns from their newspaper page and write them at the top of the reproducible. They will use those words to write a narrative. Ask students to underline or highlight the nouns as they use them. Remind them to use good writing techniques and be creative! (Emphasize any grammar or punctuation rules you may need to reinforce.)

Invite students to draw a picture to accompany their narrative in the box. When they're done writing, ask students to exchange papers with their partner so they can peer-edit each other's work.

Have students work independently on their narratives. Circulate around the room and assist as needed. Play background music (no lyrics) to enhance productivity and creativity, and set an age-appropriate time limit.

Closure

Encourage volunteers to read aloud their narratives to the class. Have students cut out the newspaper section containing their highlighted words. Ask them to glue it on sheet of poster board next to their narrative. Have students use a marker to draw a line from each noun in the newspaper to the noun in their narrative. Display student work around the room.

Independent Practice

For homework, invite students to list 20 nouns found at home. Have them break down their list into people, places, and things.

> "Talking stimulates the frontal lobe and aids in the processing of new information. This also serves as a brain break in a long lesson."

Name ______________________ Date ____________

Newspaper Narrative

Directions: Use this page to write a narrative using five chosen nouns.

Nouns: ____________ ____________ ____________

____________ ____________

Title: ______________________

978-1-4129-5272-9 • © Corwin Press

Formal or Informal . . . That Is the Question!

Standard
Adjust the use of spoken, written, and visual language (e.g., conventions, style, vocabulary) to communicate effectively with a variety of audiences and for different purposes.

Objective
Students will identify informal and formal phrases and rephrase from informal to formal register.

Anticipatory Set
Ahead of time, review the **Formal or Informal reproducible (page 15)**. Tell students you are going to read aloud a few phrases. If students think the phrase is something they should say to the president of the United States, they should stand up. If not, they should stay seated. Read the list of phrases from the reproducible.

Formal or Informal Page 15

Purpose
Discuss with students that certain words and phrases are used in everyday conversations with families and friends. These words and phrases are not formal enough to use in situations such as meeting an important adult or writing a paper for school. Tell students they are going to practice restating some informal phrases to make them more formal.

Input
Explain that we all have words or phrases we use with people who are close to us. These words are sometimes referred to as *slang* or *dialect*, and they may be different depending on where we live. For example, people from the South have ways of saying things different from people from the Pacific Coast. The way we talk to people who are close to us is called our "informal register." Informal registers are not wrong. We just have to realize that they are for informal situations.

Remind students that school is a formal setting. When students address a teacher or principal or write a paper for class, they should use words and phrases from the formal register. Formal-register words are grammatically correct and commonly understood in proper English language. Tell students they will practice using the formal register so it will be easier the next time they write a paper for school.

> Having students stand and sit is an easy way of adding blood-pumping movement to a lesson.

Say It Formally Page 16

Modeling

◄ Copy and cut apart the phrase cards on the **Say It Formally reproducible (page 16)**. Place the cards in a basket at the front of the class. Read aloud a card to students. Tell them that this is an informal phrase. If they want to use it in a paper for school, they should change it to a formal phrase. Provide an example such as changing *making my skin crawl* to *making me uneasy* or *making me uncomfortable*. If some students in your class do not have a strong command of the English language, this activity could be challenging. Model more examples as needed for understanding.

Say to students: *Each of you will take a card from the basket. Wander around the room until I give a signal (or turn off the music). At that signal, pair up with the person closest to you. Read your card to your partner, and together, come up with a more formal way to say the phrase. Then repeat the process using your partner's card.* After both cards have been read and revised, tell students to return their cards to the basket and stand back-to-back with their partners. They then repeat the whole process again.

Check for Understanding

Make sure all students understand the assignment before you begin. Check by asking a volunteer to repeat the directions, and then invite students to ask questions.

Guided Practice

Place all the phrase cards from the Say It Formally reproducible in a basket, and signal students to begin. Circulate around the classroom listening to students' responses. Offer suggestions when students seem stuck.

Closure

Have students return to their seats. Give each student a copy of the Say It Formally reproducible. Ask students to write a formal phrase under each informal phrase. Encourage them to keep this sheet in a writing folder to help them when writing papers for class.

Formal or Informal

Read these phrases aloud to students. Ask students to stand if the phrase is formal (could be said to the president) or sit if the phrase is informal (inappropriate).

1. "Hey, dude!"

2. "Good morning, Mr. President."

3. "Whatcha been up to?"

4. "It sure is cool to be here."

5. "Thank you for the invitation."

6. "How's life?"

7. "Your office is impressive."

8. "You're sure doing a great job!"

9. "I appreciate the job you are doing for our country."

10. "Keep it real!"

11. "It has been an honor to meet you."

12. "Wow, this was neat!"

Say It Formally

"That's awesome!"	"That movie was sick!"
"Sportin' some bling"	"Hey!"
"Fixin' to go"	"Making my skin crawl"
"I ain't"	"Betcha can't"
"Cool"	"Hangin' with my friends"
"Like, really"	"You wanna go?"
"Over the top"	"He went missing"
"If that ain't so"	"OK"
"Yep"	"No way!"
"Don't leave me hangin"	"Totally gross"

Reproducible   978-1-4129-5272-9 • © Corwin Press

Holiday Acrostic Poems

Standard
Conduct research on issues and interests by generating ideas and questions, and by posing problems. Gather, evaluate, and synthesize data from a variety of sources (e.g., print and nonprint texts, artifacts, people) to communicate discoveries in ways that suit the purpose and audience.

Objective
Students will research a holiday in another country and create an acrostic poem.

Anticipatory Set
Lead the class in singing a holiday song such as "Jingle Bells" or "Deck the Halls." This especially grabs children's interest if it is not near the winter holiday season.

Purpose
Tell students that in the United States, some people sing songs like "Jingle Bells" or "Deck the Halls" to celebrate the Christmas holiday. There are also special songs for Hanukkah, New Year's Eve, and other holidays. We watch fireworks on the Fourth of July, and some children dress up in costumes on Halloween. People in different countries around the world have diverse ways of celebrating many different holidays. Students are going to research a holiday celebrated in another country and write an acrostic poem to share the information.

Input
Inform students that although cultures are unique around the world, everyone celebrates special holidays and events. A fun way to learn about other cultures is to research the holidays they celebrate. Tell students they are going to research holidays from different countries using encyclopedias, trade books, the Internet, and other resources. They will take notes on an outline and then use that information to create an acrostic poem.

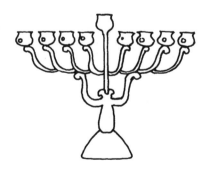

While an acrostic is a type of poetry, it is also a powerful mnemonic. Explain that an acrostic is a special kind of poem that starts with a chosen word. Each line of the poem begins with one letter of that word. Students will use the name of the country they researched to build their acrostic. The lines of the poem will include facts they learned about one of this country's holidays.

> **Mnemonics helps the brain create meaning and increase retention.**

Modeling

Model an example of an acrostic for students. Tell them you are researching Christmas in Italy. Give students a copy of the **Christmas in Italy, Holiday Research Outline** and **Christmas in Italy Acrostic reproducibles (pages 19–21)**. Tell them you are using the information on the first reproducible to take notes for your outline. Invite a volunteer to read aloud "Christmas in Italy." Then review and complete the outline with students.

Tell students they will use the information from their outlines to write their acrostics. Invite another volunteer to read aloud the Christmas in Italy Acrostic. Point out that each line of the poem begins with a letter in the word *Italy*.

Christmas in Italy Page 19

Check for Understanding

Explain research procedures to students, and give tips for taking notes. Remind them that they don't always have to write full sentences; words and phrases work just as well.

Guided Practice

Have students begin research and complete their acrostics. This activity is lengthy and may need to be divided up and completed over a couple of days. Use one day for research and outline completion and the other day for writing acrostics. Assist students as needed. Help them identify main topics and supporting details in articles.

Closure

Invite students to present their acrostics to the class. Have them share the answer to the following question with a classmate: *What was the most interesting fact you learned about your country's holiday celebration?*

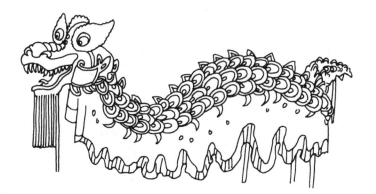

Christmas in Italy

Buon Natale!

Buon Natale!

Buon Natale!

Christmas in Italy is a holiday marked by many special days between December 6 and January 6. The most special days are Natale on December 24 and 25. This is when Italians celebrate the birth of Jesus. On December 24 most Roman Catholic families attend mass and then return home for a huge feast. The meal consists of several types of fish, pasta, and sweet breads. Children write letters to their parents telling how much they love them. They place the letters under their father's plate, and he reads them after the meal.

Family members then take turns drawing small gifts from a large, decorated bowl known as the Urn of Fate. However, most gifts are not exchanged until Epiphany on January 6. On this day, a kindly old witch named La Befana brings gifts to all good children. Some Italian families have Christmas trees. But many decorate a ceppo. A ceppo is a wooden pyramid decorated with candles and colored paper.

Name ______________________________ Date ______________

Holiday Research Outline

Directions: Use this page to write an outline from your holiday research.

Name of country: ______________________________

Name of holiday: ______________________________

Date(s) holiday is celebrated: ______________________________

What is the reason for the holiday? ______________________________

____

How is it celebrated? ______________________________

____

____

____

What special foods are eaten? ______________________________

____

Who participates in the festivities? ______________________________

____

What special events take place? ______________________________

____

Christmas in Italy Acrostic

Italians decorate wooden pyramids called ceppos with candles and colored paper.

Tables are filled with fish, pasta, and sweet breads on December 24 and 25.

All the children write letters to their parents telling how much they love them.

La Befana brings gifts to good boys and girls on January 6.

Young and old draw gifts from the Urn of Fate and wish one another "Buon Natale!"

Imagine with Nonsense

Standard

Read a wide range of print and nonprint texts to build an understanding of texts, of selves, and of the cultures of the United States and the world; to acquire new information; to respond to needs and demands of society and the workplace; and for personal fulfillment (includes fiction and nonfiction, classic, and contemporary works).

Objective

Students will work with cooperative groups to demonstrate reading fluency and create an imaginary creature.

Anticipatory Set

Read aloud a portion of Lewis Carroll's "Jabberwocky," using a great deal of expression and drama.

Purpose

Point out that this poem is filled with fun, interesting nonsense words and imagery. Students are going to use their imagination and reading skills to perform a dramatic reading of "Jabberwocky" and then create an image of this imaginary creature.

PART 1

Input

Explain that "Jabberwocky" is a poem written by a famous author and poet named Lewis Carroll. Mention books with which students might be familiar, such as *Alice's Adventures in Wonderland* and *Through the Looking Glass*. Poems like "Jabberwocky" are fun to read because the nonsense words evoke our imaginations. The whole time we are reading, our minds are trying to form an image of the Jabberwocky and where it might be lurking!

Modeling

Instruct students to watch and listen as you read aloud a portion of the poem again. Repeat the dramatic reading from the Anticipatory Set. Model tone, reading speed, and movements that make the reading more interesting and exciting.

Guided Practice

Divide the class into groups of four to six students, and assign each group a portion of the poem to present to the class. Students will also develop body movements to enhance their reading and make it more interesting to watch.

Allow students to practice so they can read with fluency. Reading fluently means that they read at an appropriate speed and with expression. Encourage group members to work together to determine how to pronounce and act out nonsense words. You may want to allow more than one day for this activity so students have time to practice at home, as well.

Finally, have groups present their poem sections in order. Videotape the presentation so students may watch the entire poem without interruption.

Closure

Invite students to watch the videotape together. Encourage them to praise each other's work and point out elements they liked from each presentation. Ask students to record their thoughts and reflections about the experience in a journal.

PART 2

Input

Congratulate students on their wonderful job performing the dramatic readings of "Jabberwocky." Explain that one of the great things about this poem is that it gives clues to the Jabberwocky's appearance, yet it also leaves much to the imagination. Inform students that they will work in groups again to create an artistic interpretation of the Jabberwocky.

Modeling

Say to students: *When I read "Jabberwocky," my mind tries to imagine what a Jabberwocky looks like. Is it sort of like a dragon? Or is it more like a giant?* Explain that each group is responsible for creating a picture of what they think the Jabberwocky looks like using torn colored tissue paper and markers.

Give each group a large piece of waxed paper and sheets of different colored tissue paper. Invite students to create a picture of the Jabberwocky using torn pieces of the tissue paper. Demonstrate how to

> **" Using imagination helps create meaning and novelty in lessons, which increases retention. "**

tear up tissue paper pieces and glue them to waxed paper. Add a few details with markers.

Check for Understanding

Make sure all groups understand the assignment before anyone begins. Encourage students to ask questions and discuss possible strategies and techniques for creating their pictures.

Guided Practice

Have students work in the same groups used for the dramatic reading. To ensure all group members participate, assign individual roles to team members such as Supply Guy and Chaos Controller, and allow only one or two team members to touch the glue. Limiting who can touch the supplies decreases the risk of one person doing all the work.

Distribute supplies and play background music (no lyrics) to enhance creativity. Allow about 30–40 minutes for the activity.

When they're finished, help students attach their Jabberwocky pictures to windows around the room. When the sunlight hits the pictures, they will shine like stained-glass windows!

Closure

Allow groups to share their creations with the class. Encourage them to point out what parts of the poem inspired their Jabberwocky's appearance.

Extend the Activity

Invite students to use the **My Nonsense Poem reproducible (page 25)** to write poems imitating Lewis Carroll's style and use of nonsense words. Have them write about their own original creature and give it an interesting, nonsense name. Poems can be rhymed or freeform. Encourage students to use fun, imaginative nonsense words, just like Carroll. Ask volunteers to read aloud their poems to the class.

My Nonsense Poem Page 25

Name ______________________ Date ______________

My Nonsense Poem

Directions: Write your own nonsense poem on the lines below. Use your imagination and be creative!

My Creature's Name: ______________________

CHAPTER 2

Mathematics

> **You cannot recall information that your brain does not retain.**

Mathematics is often the least favorite subject for both students and teachers. A common misconception about math is that facts and figures can't be fun, so lecture is often the primary strategy used to impart this wisdom on the next generation. Lecture, however, has been proven the least effective method for long-term retention. It's no wonder students develop a disdain for math, as it's difficult to like something you struggle to retain.

The following activities are proof that mathematics objectives can be taught in brain-compatible ways and can actually be (dare we say it?) fun! Because math concepts on paper are abstract, one of the easiest ways to make them more brain-compatible is to make them concrete by using movement and manipulatives.

A math journal is a great way to help students reflect on the concepts taught during math instruction. Taking time to reflect on new learning or applying new concepts to promote higher-order thinking can enhance retention of material and be accomplished effectively in a journal.

Show Me Y!

Standard
Algebra—Use mathematical models to represent and understand quantitative relationships.

Objective
Students will use their bodies to form the answers to given equations.

Anticipatory Set
Write the following sentence frame on the board: *We go to school five _____ per week.* Ask students to read the sentence and think about what word would most logically complete it. Tell them to whisper their answer to a classmate, and invite a volunteer to provide the answer. While a few words might fit, the most logical answer is *days*.

Purpose
Explain to students that they are used to thinking of language in terms of sentences, but mathematics also has a form of sentence called an *equation*. An equation is a number sentence. Students will practice completing math equations just like they completed the other sentence.

Input
Inform students that math sentences, or equations, are written so the numbers on one side equal the numbers on the other side. Write the following sentence on the board: *Four times three equals twelve.*

Explain that writing equations this way is too long, so mathematicians developed symbols to represent words in math sentences. This same sentence can also be written as $4 \times 3 = 12$.

Even though it looks a little different, it is read from left to right just like an English sentence. If words or symbols are left out of a math equation, students can use their knowledge of math and equation structure to figure out the missing piece. Write the following equation on the board: $4 \times \_\_\_\_\_ = 12$.

> **Retention rates are highest at the beginning of a lesson. Therefore, it is important to give accurate information rather than allow students to guess answers.**

Propose that the number *3* most logically fits in the blank because it makes both sides of the = sign the same. Mathematicians often substitute letters, such as *y*, in place of the blank line. This letter, called a *variable*, represents the number that completes the equation. Write the following equation on the board: $4 \times y = 12$. Students would solve the problem the same way they did before.

To solve this equation, students must ask themselves what number multiplied by 4 equals 12. The answer is 3. All they have to do is figure out what number the letter represents. Students will play a game to practice figuring out what *y* stands for in multiplication equations.

Modeling

Tell students you are going to write an equation with a missing number on the board. You will write *y* to represent the missing number. Students will work in teams to figure out what number *y* represents. Then they will use their bodies to show the missing number. Model the following example:

Write $2 \times y = 8$ on the board. Ask students: *What number would make this equation correct? Talk it over with your team, but don't say the answer. You will show me the answer using your bodies. Be creative! Decide with your teammates how you can show the answer 4.* Describe several examples, such as: *Form your bodies into the shape of a 4; have four students stand up; hold out four hands or four feet.* The group that shows the correct answer first gets a point, and a point will also be awarded to the group that shows the answer in the most creative way. After you write each equation on the board, tell students not to move or say anything until you give the signal: *Show me Y!*

Check for Understanding

Check to make sure everyone understands the activity. Repeat that you will write an equation on the board. It will have a missing number represented by the letter *y*. Students will work with their teams to show what *y* represents. Model more examples as needed.

Guided Practice

One at a time, write the equations from the **Show Me Y! reproducible (page 30)** on the board. Remember to allow discussion time before giving the signal, *Show me Y!* Keep track of each group's points. Take away points from groups that move or talk before you give the signal. Praise groups that are working together well.

Show Me Y! Page 30

Closure

Award the winning teams small, simple prizes. After students return to their seats, give them a copy of the Show Me Y! reproducible. Have them complete the page so they can recall the information they just presented. Instruct students to answer the question on the bottom of the page in their math journals.

Independent Practice

Reinforce the concept of using variables by having students complete the **Give Me a Y! reproducible (page 31)** for homework.

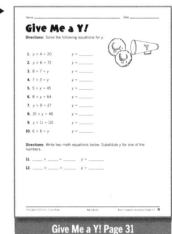

Give Me a Y! Page 31

Show Me Y!

Directions: Solve the following equations for *y*.

1. $7 \times y = 28$ *y* = _____

2. $3 \times y = 15$ *y* = _____

3. $y \times 6 = 54$ *y* = _____

4. $y \times 6 = 18$ *y* = _____

5. $2 \times 4 = y$ *y* = _____

6. $8 \times 2 = y$ *y* = _____

7. $3 \times y = 24$ *y* = _____

8. $y \times 5 = 35$ *y* = _____

9. $6 \times 7 = y$ *y* = _____

10. $y \times 5 = 20$ *y* = _____

Directions: Answer the following questions.

A math equation is like a sentence because _____

_____

A math equation is *not* like a sentence because _____

_____

Give Me a Y!

Directions: Solve the following equations for y.

1. $y \times 4 = 20$ y = _____

2. $y \times 6 = 72$ y = _____

3. $8 \times 7 = y$ y = _____

4. $7 \times 3 = y$ y = _____

5. $5 \times y = 45$ y = _____

6. $8 \times y = 64$ y = _____

7. $y \times 9 = 27$ y = _____

8. $10 \times y = 40$ y = _____

9. $y \times 11 = 121$ y = _____

10. $6 \times 6 = y$ y = _____

Directions: Write two math equations below. Substitute y for one of the numbers.

11. _____ $\times$ _____ = _____   y = _____

12. _____ $\times$ _____ = _____   y = _____

Build It Write

Standard

Geometry—Use visualization, spatial reasoning, and geometric modeling to solve problems.

Objective

Students will create a two-dimensional geometric shape from pattern blocks and describe its construction in an expository paragraph using correct terminology.

Anticipatory Set

Set up a simple maze in the classroom. Blindfold a student volunteer, and have him or her try to get through the maze using only your verbal commands. Repeat with a couple more volunteers. Ask students: *How important was it that my verbal commands were correct? What might have happened if I used words you could not understand or if I had left out a step?* Allow students to respond.

Purpose

Tell students that using correct terminology and performing steps in the appropriate order are also very important in math. For this activity, they will practice using the correct terminology for geometric shapes and writing steps in logical order to create a design.

Input

Although most students are familiar with the shapes used in pattern blocks, they often refer to them using incorrect names. Using a set of pattern blocks or shapes cut from construction paper, review the mathematical names of geometric shapes. Hold up each piece as you say its name: *This is a **square**; this is a **hexagon**; this is a **triangle**; this is a **trapezoid**; this is a **rhombus**.*

Tell students that if they want to write instructions for how to build a design with pattern blocks, they would use a special type of writing called *expository writing*. Explain that expository writing describes how to do something. When writing instructions, it is important that steps are listed in logical or sequential order and that correct terminology is used.

Modeling

Give students one hexagon, one square, one trapezoid, one triangle, one rhombus, and a copy of the **Pattern Block Design reproducible (page 34)**. This page shows an example of expository writing describing how to build a design with pattern blocks. Place a transparency of the reproducible on the overhead, and read it to students. Ask students to listen and read along.

Invite students to try to create the design you just described using their pattern blocks. Then demonstrate on the overhead using transparent pattern blocks, or draw the design step by step. Inform students that the quality of the instructions in the expository paragraph determines how similar their designs will be to yours. Writing a paragraph for others to follow is harder than it appears! Tell students they will have the opportunity to practice this skill.

Pattern Block Design Page 34

Check for Understanding

Ask a volunteer to repeat the directions for the activity to ensure that everyone understands. Remind students to use correct terminology for the blocks and put the steps in logical, sequential order.

Guided Practice

Have students design an original geometric shape using pattern blocks. Allow them access to at least two of each geometric shape. When they're done with their design, they will write an expository paragraph describing how to build it.

Allow students to go to different areas of the room to keep their designs secret and write their paragraphs. Assist as needed. Then have students exchange papers with a partner to see if they can follow the directions to build the design.

Closure

Have students ask their partners how they could make their paragraph easier to read. *Did they miss any steps? Did they use directional words such as **left** and **right** or sequential terms such as **first** and **next**?* Ask students to take notes in their math journals.

Independent Practice

For homework, have students use their notes to rewrite their expository paragraphs. Assess students based on your ability to read the paragraph and effectively create the design. Have students trace and color their designs and attach their paragraphs.

> **The use of manipulatives adds a kinesthetic and visual component, which can increase retention rates in a variety of learners.**

Pattern Block Design

To make my secret pattern block design, follow these directions. First, place the hexagon on a flat surface. Second, place one side of a square against the top side of the hexagon. Third, place the shorter top side of the trapezoid against the bottom side of the hexagon. Next, place one angle of a triangle against the right side angle of the hexagon.

Finally, get two rhombuses. Place the acute angle of one rhombus against the top right angle of the square. Position the rhombus at an angle. Place the acute angle of the other rhombus against the top left angle of the square. Position the rhombus at any angle.

Make this design in the box below. What do you see?

Project Big Print

Standard

Measurement—Understand measurable attributes of objects and the units, systems, and processes of measurement.

Objective

Students will discover the value of standard measurement.

Anticipatory Set

Read the text at the top of the **Project Big Print reproducible (page 37)** to students as though you were reading the details of a mission to a group of top-secret scientists. To enhance motivation and novelty, treat students as though they are on a secret mission throughout the lesson.

Purpose

Tell students that they are on a mission. Their mission is to locate the latest Big Foot footprint and measure it with given "scientific" instruments.

Input

Inform students that it is imperative to have two independent investigations. Each team will be given one footprint model to measure. Students will need to keep their measurements and instruments secret from the other team until they report their findings to you.

Modeling

Place a transparency of the Project Big Print reproducible on an overhead, and give a copy to each student. Go over the reproducible so students know how to complete it. Say only that *P* is the unit of measurement they will use. Each team will receive a bag containing "lab equipment"—measuring devices and pencils. They will use the measuring device in the bag to measure their footprint. Students will have ten minutes to complete their investigation and record their findings.

Demonstrate how to measure the footprint using a nonstandard measuring tool, such as a pencil, crayon, or piece of chalk. Write your measurement on the transparency.

Project Big Print Page 37

> **Novelty and motivation are both linked to increased retention rates.**

Check for Understanding

Ask students: *Does everyone understand your mission? You will measure your assigned Big Foot print using your lab equipment and record the data on your lab sheet. Remember, it's important for the integrity of the mission that each team keeps all data and instruments a secret until the findings are reported!*

Guided Practice

Divide the class into two teams. Give one team a bag containing pencils and pretzel rods. Give the other team a bag containing pencils and pretzel sticks. Place enlarged copies of the footprint cut from the **Big Foot Footprint reproducible (page 38)** in two different locations in the classroom. Try to put the prints far enough apart so the teams cannot see each other's measuring instruments. Give students ten minutes to complete the assignment.

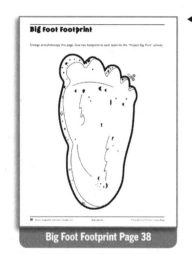

Big Foot Footprint Page 38

Closure

When teams are done, have them place equipment back in their bags and return to their seats. Place the Project Big Print transparency on the overhead so teams can analyze their data. Ask one member of each team to report their measurement. Write responses on the overhead. (The team with pretzel rods should have a much lower number than the team with pretzel sticks.) Tell students that you can't report your findings until both teams agree on one measurement. Ask: *How do you think your data could be so different?*

Ask students to empty their equipment bags, and allow them to discover what caused the different measurements—different-sized pretzels, or measuring tools. Ask students how they can ensure that people come up with the same measurements. Guide them to recognize the value of standard measurements and measuring tools.

Then have teams measure their Big Foot prints again using a ruler. They should report very similar or identical findings. Have students reflect on the following question in their math journals: *Why is standard measurement important?*

INDEPENDENT PRACTICE

Invite students to use different measuring instruments at home to measure the size of their room, bed, couch, or even a pet! Students can use shoes, pencils, books, combs, and more to measure objects. Invite them to report their findings to the class.

Project Big Print

Directions: Use this sheet to record your measurement of Big Foot's footprint.

Mission Notes

During a recent expedition, top-secret scientists made an amazing discovery! This discovery might end the legendary debate over Big Foot. A large footprint was found and has been carefully preserved for scientific study. Your top-secret mission is to measure the print and record your results on this lab sheet. It is very important that all records be kept secret until we can find out if these prints are real. Your government is counting on you!

Name: _____

Code Name: _____

Print Measurements:

_____

P1 (length)

_____

P2 (width)

CONFIDENTIAL

Big Foot Footprint

Enlarge and photocopy this page. Give two footprints to each team for the Project Big Print activity.

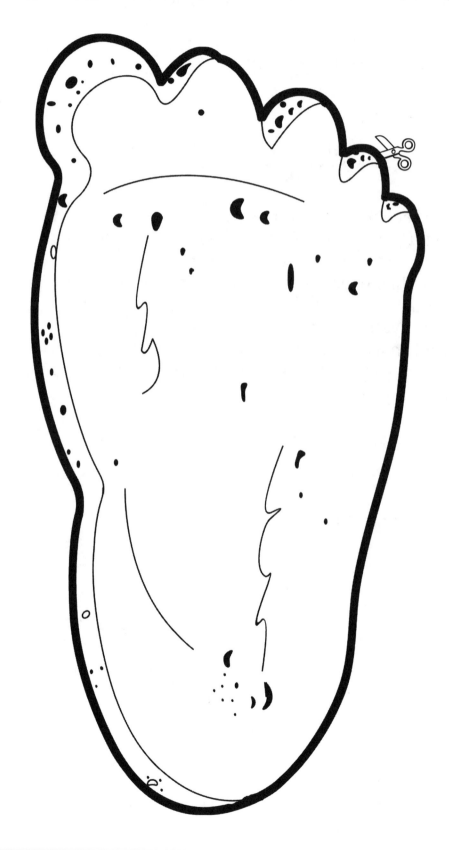

Reproducible 978-1-4129-5272-9 • © Corwin Press

Where's the Acorn?

Standard
Numbers and Operations—Understand numbers, ways of representing numbers, relationships among numbers, and number systems.

Objective
Students will explore integers less than zero by using visuals to move up and down the number line.

Anticipatory Set
Using the **Find the Acorn 1 reproducible (page 41)** as a guide, draw a large tree on a sheet of butcher paper. The tree should extend an equal distance up to the limbs as it does down to the roots. Draw a vertical number line on the tree so zero is at ground level, 10 is near the top of the tree, and –10 is at the bottom of the roots.

    Call students' attention to the tree. Tell them to picture it in their minds, with a squirrel running up and down the trunk. Now tell them to imagine that a huge storm blew the tree down on its side. (Reposition the tree so that it is lying on its side, with positive integers to the right and negative integers to the left.)

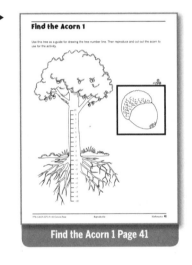

Find the Acorn 1 Page 41

Purpose
Tell students that they will try to help the squirrel find acorns it has hidden in different places up and down the tree.

Input
Explain the difference between positive and negative numbers. Point out *0* in the center of the tree trunk, with numbers continuing on either side. Numbers to the right of 0 on the tree are called *positive numbers*. Numbers to the left of 0 are called *negative numbers*.

    Explain that negative numbers have a subtraction sign in front to remind us that they are less than 0. Point to several negative numbers as examples. Negative numbers continue in the same order as positive numbers but in the opposite direction.

Modeling
In this activity, students will visualize numbers on the number line. When you ask a question, they will visualize the answer. When you say *buddy check*, students whisper the answer to a partner. When partners both agree on the answer, they write it down. You will then call on

> **Metaphors can help students establish meaning for new learning.**

volunteers to place an acorn on the number tree where they think it is located. Model a couple of examples for students.

Model the following: *Start on 7, and go left seven places. Picture the number tree and the answer in your head.* (Allow thinking time.) *Now, buddy check!* (Allow time for students to confer with partners.) *You should put the acorn here on 0.* (Place the acorn on 0.) *The answer is 0, because seven places to the left of 7 is 0.*

Model another example: *Start on 7 again, but this time move nine places to the left. Think of your answer.* (Allow thinking time.) *Now, buddy check!* (Allow time for students to confer with partners.) *This time, the acorn should be on –2, because nine places to the left of 7 is –2.* (Place the acorn on –2.)

Check for Understanding

Allow students to confirm that they understand each step of the instructions. Ask volunteers to repeat the steps back to you, or have them show "thumbs up" or "thumbs down" to demonstrate they understand how to proceed.

Guided Practice

Find the Acorn 2 Page 42

Divide the class into groups of two or three students. Read aloud the problems from the **Find the Acorn 2 reproducible (page 42)**. Remember to allow plenty of time for students to confer with their partners. Call on random student pairs to share their answers and place an acorn in the correct spot on the tree.

Closure

Guide a discussion about positive and negative numbers. Ask students how the tree image helped them remember which numbers go up and which numbers go down. Have students answer the following question in their math journals: *What is another way you can remember that positive numbers go up and negative numbers go down?*

Independent Practice

Have students complete the **Surfing the Number Line reproducible (page 43)** for homework. Remind them that they are using a number line instead of a number tree. Encourage them to think of the tree or another visual to help answer the questions.

Find the Acorn 1

Use this tree as a guide for drawing the tree number line. Then reproduce and cut out the acorn to use for the activity.

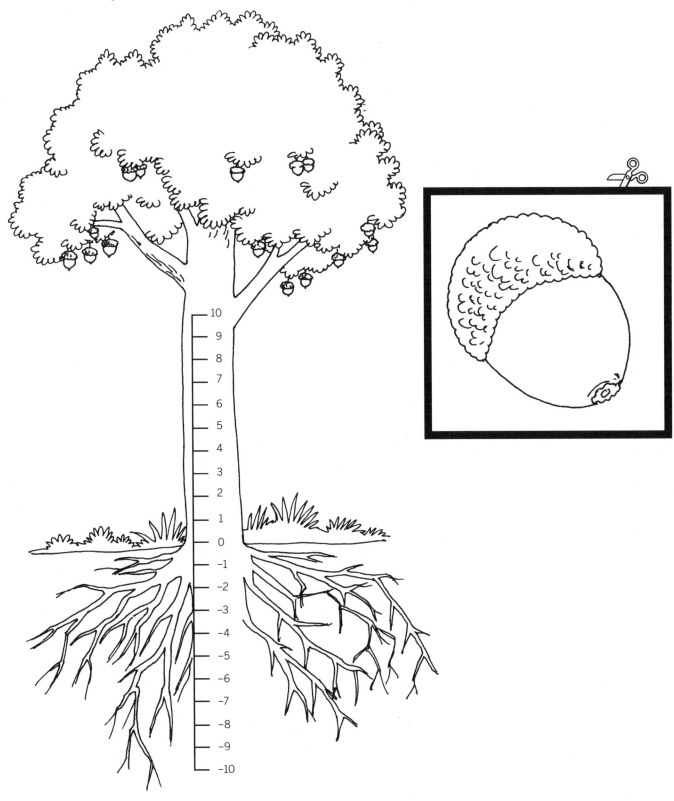

Find the Acorn 2

Read aloud the following problems to students. Encourage them to visualize the number line to solve the problems.

1. Start at 6, and go down 3. Where's the acorn?

2. Start at 3, and go down 4. Where's the acorn?

3. Start at –1, and go down 6. Where's the acorn?

4. Start at –7, and go up 2. Where's the acorn?

5. Start at –5, and go up 5. Where's the acorn?

6. Start at 0, and go up 4. Where's the acorn?

7. Start at 4, and go up 6. Where's the acorn?

8. Start at 10, and go down 8. Where's the acorn?

9. Start at 2, and go down 4. Where's the acorn?

10. Start at –2, and go down 6. Where's the acorn?

11. Start at –4, and go up 12. Where's the acorn?

12. Start at 3, and go down 7. Where's the acorn?

Surfing the Number Line

Directions: Use the number line to help you find the answers.

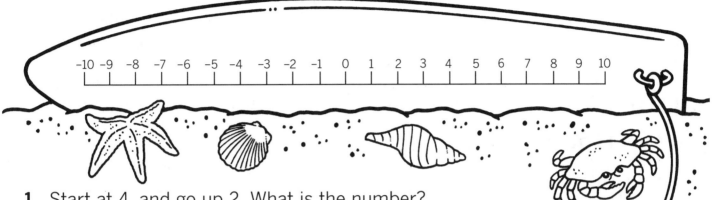

-10 -9 -8 -7 -6 -5 -4 -3 -2 -1 0 1 2 3 4 5 6 7 8 9 10

1. Start at 4, and go up 2. What is the number? _____

2. Start at –3, and go down 4. What is the number? _____

3. Start at –6, and go up 7. What is the number? _____

4. Start at 5, and go down 3. What is the number? _____

5. Start at –2, and go down 8. What is the number? _____

6. Start at 8, and go down 13. What is the number? _____

Directions: Use the number line to help you find the answers. Start each new line with the previous answer.

7. Start with 0, and go up 2. What is the number? _____

8. Start with _____, and go down 4. What is the number? _____

9. Start with _____, and go down 3. What is the number? _____

10. Start with _____, and go up 8. What is the number? _____

11. Start with _____, and go up 5. What is the number? _____

12. Start with _____, and go down 8. The number should be 0!

CHAPTER 3

Social Studies

> **Learning and retention are different. We can learn something for just a few minutes then lose it forever.**

Social studies objectives lend themselves to brain-compatible teaching strategies. However, it is difficult for teachers to determine the main concepts on which to focus. Social studies texts, while a helpful resource, are filled with minute details that may not be vital to a student's understanding of the main ideas. If we want students to retain the information long-term, we have to be aware of how short- and long-term memory work. The brain of a young child can process only about five to seven chunks of new information at a time. Therefore, if we want students to remember what we teach them, we have to limit the amount of material we cover and find ways to help them better retain that material. The idea is to do a better job of teaching less.

Students can learn facts and information and hold the memory long enough to take a test. Retaining the information requires the learner to give conscious attention to facts and build conceptual frameworks to move the information into long-term memory. In social studies, students are often required to memorize important dates, names of people, and significant places. Rote rehearsal helps students remember facts for tests. Elaborative rehearsal, in which students reprocess the information numerous times, requires students to discover relationships, make associations with prior learning, and interpret meaning. Elaborative rehearsal will help students remember those important dates, people, and places for much longer than next week's test.

Concept maps and visualization are great ways to help students make sense of new learning in social studies. Brain-compatible social studies instruction is as much fun for teachers as it is for students. Just remember, less is more!

Social Studies Comic Strip

Standard
Activity can align with any standard, depending on the content of the text.

Objective
Students will outline a chapter of a social studies text using visuals.

Anticipatory Set
Read an age-appropriate comic strip to students. Make transparencies of the comic strip so students can see the pictures as well as hear the text.

Purpose
Tell students that comic strips are fun to read because they tell a story using both pictures and words. They are going to work together to create a comic strip that tells the main ideas in a chapter from their social studies text.

Input
Ask students if they like to read newspaper comic strips, also known as "the funnies." Discuss comic strip features with students. Comic strips are not very long, so cartoonists must be careful to include only the most important ideas in a joke or story. They must also consider how they can use pictures and words together to convey the most information in a limited space. We know what happens first, second, and third because the pictures are in boxes, or cells, that read in order from left to right. A comic strip is a type of concept map, or flowchart, which is useful for helping organize information in logical order.

> **Visualization of new concepts helps establish meaning and increase retention.**

Explain that social studies texts contain a lot of information but that some is more important than others. Students' objective is to create a comic strip, or flowchart, that conveys the main idea of a chapter from their social studies text.

Modeling

Model how to create a comic strip cell. Begin by reading aloud the first section of the social studies chapter students are currently studying. Guide students in finding the main idea. On an overhead projector, draw a cartoon-like picture in a box, or cell, that conveys the main idea. Use both pictures and words in speech balloons.

Check for Understanding

Ask students if they understand the activity. Before drawing, they should brainstorm the best way to convey the main idea. Remind students that they may use words in speech bubbles but the picture should tell most of the story.

Guided Practice

◀ Give students a copy of the **Social Studies Comic Strip reproducible (page 47)**, and assign sections of your current social studies chapter to individuals or student pairs. Each student or pair is responsible for creating one cell for a comic strip that conveys the main idea of his or her section.

While students create their comic strip, play background music (no lyrics) to enhance creativity and productivity. If you have any music that reflects a culture or place you are studying, even better! Assist students as needed, making sure they cover the main ideas. When students are finished, have them cut the box from the reproducible and wait for further instructions.

Social Studies Comic Strip Page 47

Closure

Invite students to present their comic strip cells, in order, to the class. Ask each student to point out how he or she represented the main idea. Then display all the cells along a wall to form a complete comic strip, or flowchart. Encourage students to use the comic strip as a study guide for future tests.

Independent Practice

For the next social studies chapter, ask students to outline it using pictures and a flowchart. Remind them to feature only the main ideas.

Name _____ Date _____

Social Studies Comic Strip

Directions: Record notes from the social studies book.

Chapter title: _____

My section of the chapter: _____

The main idea is: _____

A Different Perspective

Standard

Understand relationships among science, technology, and society.

Objective

Students will write and present a play about the completion of the transcontinental railroad in the United States.

Anticipatory Set

Read the poem from the **"Imagine, if You Will" reproducible (page 51)**, or show a clip from a video that features a well-known story from a different perspective.

Purpose

Tell students they are going to learn about an important event in American history. They will write a play about this event to present to their classmates. The perspective of the play, however, will be rather unique. Students will have to think like a mouse or some other animal!

Railroad Article Page 52

Input

Explain that the completion of the transcontinental railroad was a huge milestone in U.S. history. People and goods were able to travel across the country by train for the first time. The West was officially open for business!

◄ Give students a copy of the **Railroad Article reproducible (page 52)**. Explain that this is a newspaper article describing the events of that historic day. Students are going to use the article to help research facts for their play.

PART 1

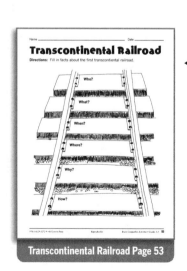
Transcontinental Railroad Page 53

Modeling

◄ Give students a copy of the **Transcontinental Railroad reproducible (page 53)**, and place a transparency of the reproducible on the overhead. Explain that this worksheet will help them organize information from the article in a way their brains can remember. Point out the title at the top of the page and the connecting boxes labeled *who, what, when, where, why,* and *how*. Students will work with a partner to answer each question in the appropriate box.

Model for students how to complete the reproducible. Select a student volunteer as your partner. Ask your partner to read aloud the first sentence in the newspaper article. Stop him or her, and say: *I think I heard where the two railroads met to form the transcontinental railroad. It said the transcontinental railroad was completed in Promontory Summit, Utah. Do you agree? Let's write that in the* **Where** *section.* Demonstrate on the overhead.

Explain that partners then switch roles and the other student reads. Continue back and forth until all the questions on the page are answered.

Check for Understanding

Make sure students understand the reading and questioning procedure. Go over the strategy again as needed.

Guided Practice

Pair off students, and send them to different areas of the classroom to complete the activity. Remind them to practice good listening skills and to take turns. If students finish before you call *Time*, ask them to go back and see if they can add details to each answer.

Closure

Have students wander around the classroom and find a new partner. Ask them to compare concept maps with their new partners and add any missing details. Then have students return to their seats.

PART 2

Modeling

Tell students they are now experts on the completion of the transcontinental railroad. They will use that information to write a play from a unique perspective—some kind of animal family living under the railroad! This animal family has just discovered a golden spike in their living room. Explain that through play dialogue, students will tell all the facts they wrote on their concept map from the animal family's perspective.

Using a mouse family as an example, ask students: *How do you think the mice felt when they discovered the spike? Do you think there might have been a lot of noise in their home during the last few days? Tell*

> **Concept maps help students chunk information in memorable patterns.**

their story in your play. Use a simple mouse puppet to model a possible response to the golden spike: *Look at this beautiful golden tree root! I might like it if it weren't in the middle of my living room. Maybe we should decorate it! Maybe it's a sign of good things to come! Is it edible? What does it taste like? What does it feel like? What should we do with it?*

Guided Practice

Instruct students to work in small groups to write a play, make puppets, and present the finished product. Each group member must write and present at least two lines in the play, and all the major facts from the concept map must be included. After students finish writing their play, they will make puppets and practice.

Provide them with socks and various art supplies to make simple animal puppets. Play background music (no lyrics) to enhance creativity and productivity. Students may need to work on this project for a couple of days in order to have ample time to write, practice, and create puppets.

Have student groups present their plays to the class. If possible, place a table at the front of the class. Hang butcher paper or a sheet from the table's front and sides to make a puppet stage. Encourage students to watch politely while each group presents their play and to praise one another's creativity.

Directions for Sock Puppets

Use an old sock as a base. Glue wiggly eyes approximately two inches from the toe line. Cut and glue yarn for hair. Add ears, mouth, and a nose with felt scraps, and add details with markers. If you wish, make clothing out of scrap fabric.

Closure

Discuss with students how different perspectives can change how we view the same event. Invite volunteers to share the ways each play showed a unique perspective.

Independent Practice

Have students summarize the major facts from their completed Transcontinental Railroad reproducible in a paragraph.

Imagine, if You Will...

Imagine, if you will...
A date from history,
Maybe the day a war was won
Or our country became free.

Now imagine, if you will...
A different point of view.
Events may have another feel
If suddenly you weren't you.

The Boston Tea Party is a time
Not remembered with such glee
If, instead of a disguised patriot,
You were a box of tea.

Circling the wagons was a great defense
That pioneers would brag on,
But it might not seem so all-fire great
If you were the wagon.

The Pony Express was a great system.
It helped us talk, of course.
But consider how your mind might change
If you were the horse.

Events that happen are often recalled
Differently, it's true.
But we can better understand each other
When we see different points of view.

Name _____ Date _____

Railroad Article

Herald News

GOLDEN SPIKE CONNECTS COUNTRY!

May 10, 1869, Promontory Summit, Utah:

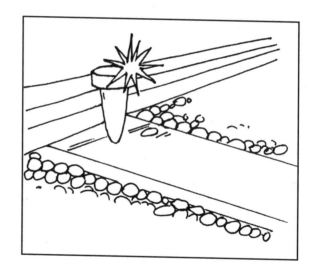

The Central Pacific Railroad and the Union Pacific Railroad were connected today, forming the first transcontinental railroad in the United States. A golden spike was used to connect the final rails in Promontory Summit, Utah. The new transcontinental line runs 3,500 miles from New York to California. This new line will enable passengers to travel across the country in just six days, as opposed to the perilous six-month journey pioneers made over land. It took both companies several years and many thousands of workers to complete the task.

Transcontinental Railroad

Directions: Fill in facts about the first transcontiental railroad.

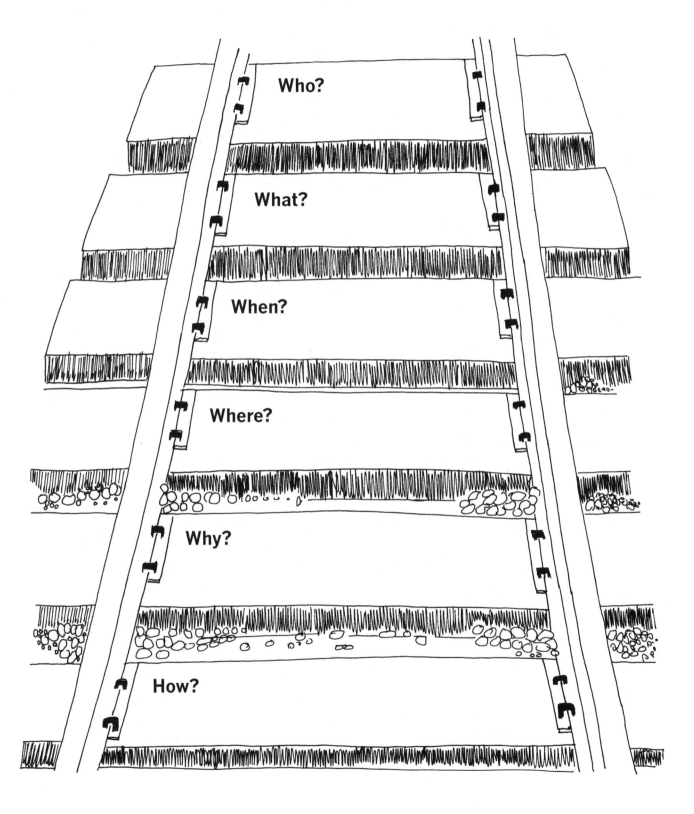

Who?

What?

When?

Where?

Why?

How?

Good Character Medal

Standard

Understand individual development and identity.

Objective

Students will create a medal that promotes their good character traits.

Anticipatory Set

Describe to students someone you admire, such as Martin Luther King, Jr., Abraham Lincoln, Harriet Tubman, or even a relative or friend. Describe the good qualities these people possess. Invite students to share the names of people they admire and describe their good qualities.

Purpose

A person's good qualities are positive character traits. Everyone has good character traits, whether they are famous or the person living next door. Students will consider their best character traits and design a medal that represents those traits.

Input

Explain to students the meaning of the word *character*. Character describes someone's qualities, like integrity, good manners, kindness, or generosity. Tell students you will be holding a Character Awards Ceremony in which students are rewarded for their good character. They have been chosen out of thousands of applicants to be celebrated today. Students will each receive a medal highlighting their best qualities! Unfortunately, the company sent blank medals and lost the list of qualities for which each student won the award. Tell students you need their help to get the medals finished in time for the awards ceremony.

Ask each student to list several examples of good character traits on sticky notes. While students are writing, draw a Good Character word web on chart paper. Invite students to stick their notes on the web. Examples might include: *friendly, honest, positive, strong, caring, giving, supportive, hard working,* and *helpful.* Read examples from the chart.

Ask students to come to the chart one by one and take two to three sticky notes. Instruct students to find one note that describes themselves. They will stick the other notes on classmates who exhibit those traits. After students give out all their sticky notes, have them return to their seats.

> "Having students get up and place a sticky note on a chart in front of the room is a great way to get blood pumping to the brain."

Modeling

Tell students: *Now each of you know at least one character trait that either you see in yourself or others see in you. Use that trait to design your Good Character medal.* Place a transparency of the **Good Character Medal reproducible (page 56)** on the overhead. Draw pictures and write words or phrases that represent one of your character traits (e.g., a top hat with the caption *Honest Abe Award for Honesty*).

Good Character Medal Page 56

Check for Understanding

Make sure students understand that they are making a medal for themselves that celebrates one of their good character traits. Model more examples as needed.

Guided Practice

Give each student a copy of the Good Character Medal reproduced on tag board. Play upbeat, inspiring background music (no lyrics) to enhance creativity. Set a timer with an age-appropriate amount of time to ensure accountability. Have students design and decorate their medals using a variety of art supplies, such as colored glue, puffy paint, markers, stickers, and glitter. Encourage students to be creative with their captions, perhaps integrating rhymes or alliteration.

Closure

Close the activity by conducting an Awards Ceremony in which you formally present each student's medal. Celebrate with an "after the show" party!

Independent Practice

Have students write a paragraph describing their chosen character trait, including specific instances when they have demonstrated that trait. Encourage them to recognize and point out when classmates demonstrate good character traits throughout the year.

Good Character Medal

Directions: Cut out the medal. Decorate it to show one of your good character traits.

Show Me the Money

Standard
Understand how people organize for the production, distribution, and consumption of goods and services.

Objective
Students will apply knowledge of modes-of-exchange vocabulary.

Anticipatory Set
Ask a student with a new pencil to trade it for a short, used pencil with no eraser. When the student refuses ask: *Why not?* The student will probably respond that it is not a fair trade.

Purpose
Tell students that they are going to learn about various forms of trade and currency and then play a game to help remember new vocabulary.

Input
Explain that the ways people get the goods and services they need to survive are called *modes of exchange*. There are three main types of exchange. Ask three volunteers to help you demonstrate these concepts. Give students a copy of the **Modes of Exchange reproducible (page 60)** to follow ▶ along during the lesson.

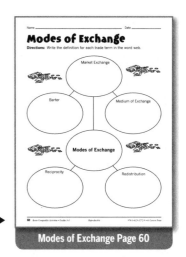

Modes of Exchange Page 60

Reciprocity The first term is *reciprocity*. Basically, it means sharing. Tell students to write *sharing* in the Reciprocity circle. Then ask your three volunteers to come to the front of the class. Give one student some apples (the farmer), one a medical bag or stethoscope (the doctor), and one a hammer (the builder). Tell students that in cultures that use reciprocity, goods and services are shared. The person who grows the food, for example, gives some to those who don't. Have the "farmer" give apples to the "doctor" and the "builder." Explain that

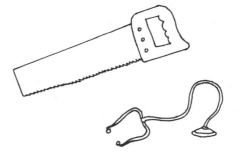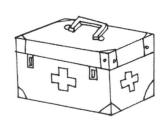

people who perform services do so as needed. Have the doctor treat the farmer and the builder act like he or she is building a house. The problem with reciprocity, however, is that some people are better at sharing than others, and some people may not be able to get what they need.

> **Visualizing new concepts can drastically increase retention.**

Redistribution The next form of exchange is *redistribution*. Redistribution is a form of exchange in which goods and services are controlled by a person or institution. Materials are distributed as needed to the people. In the Redistribution circle, have students write *Leader keeps everything and then distributes it to the people.* Ask your volunteers to distribute their apples and services to different students in the room. Explain that the problem with redistribution is that the leader or institution might not be fair. Tell the farmer to give apples only to the girls in the class.

Market Exchange The last form of exchange was created to try to help with problems in the other two. It is called *market exchange,* and there are two types.

Barter One type of market exchange is *barter*. In a barter system, goods and services are exchanged based on trading one for another. Tell students to write *trading* in the Barter circle on their reproducible. Demonstrate the barter system by having your volunteers negotiate a trade for their goods and services. For example, the farmer might offer two apples to the doctor to treat a sore toe, and the doctor might give a bottle of medicine to the builder to fix his or her roof.

Medium of Exchange Because barter does not always work for everyone, more advanced cultures developed a medium of exchange that can be applied to all services—*money*. Tell students to write *money* in the Medium of Exchange circle on their reproducible. Explain that now the farmer can sell apples for money he or she can use to pay the builder and the doctor. Give your volunteers some play money so they can demonstrate the concept.

Modeling

Pair up students with partners. Try to mix ability levels. Tell students they are going to practice and apply the new trade terms. Give each student four index cards. Have students write one term on the front of each card. On the back, have students rewrite definitions from the reproducible and draw a picture that helps them remember what they mean.

Model for students by writing *reciprocity* on an index card. On the back, write *sharing*, and draw a picture of two stick people with arrows going back and forth between them showing they are sharing. Allow students to suggest other ways you can show the concept.

Invite students to use the cards to understand these new concepts. You will read an example of a mode of exchange while students decide if it is reciprocity, redistribution, barter, or mode of exchange. Tell students to choose the card with the answer and check answers with a partner. When both partners agree, one student holds up the answer card.

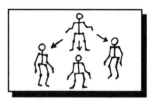

Model the activity by providing an example, such as neighbors who work together to provide different foods for the community. Emphasize that everyone shares goods. Hold up your *reciprocity* card and invite students to do the same.

Check for Understanding
Check that everyone understands how to play the game. Make sure each student has a partner and four answer cards with words, definitions, and examples.

Guided Practice
Begin by reading aloud the first scenario from the **Terms of Trade reproducible (page 61)**. Ask students: *Which term best describes the scenario I just read? Pick your card and check with your partner. Hold your card in the air when you agree.* Allow students time to confer with partners. When all students have shown their answer cards, ask a volunteer to explain his or her choice. *(The farmers are sharing.)*

Continue reading the scenarios from the reproducible, allowing time for students to choose cards and confer with partners.

Terms of Trade Page 61

Closure
Ask students to write an example of each mode of exchange on the matching card.

Independent Practice
For homework, have students create a T-chart listing the pros and cons of one mode of exchange discussed in this lesson.

Modes of Exchange

Directions: Write the definition for each trade term in the word web.

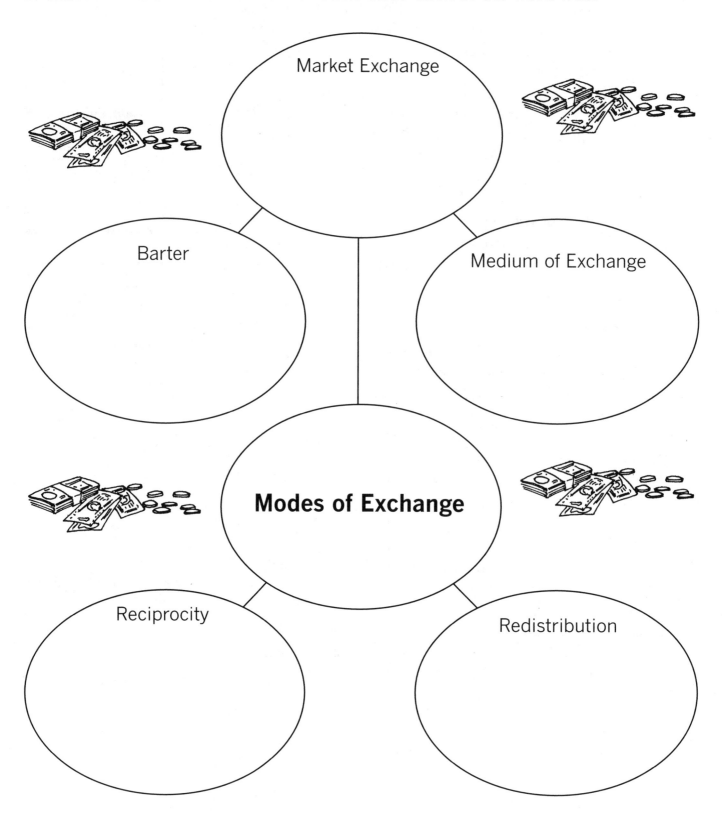

Market Exchange

Barter

Medium of Exchange

Modes of Exchange

Reciprocity

Redistribution

Terms of Trade

Read aloud the following scenarios to students for the Show Me the Money activity.

1. Two farmers live next to one another on adjoining farms. One farmer raises chickens and the other farmer plants crops. They share with one another so both have eggs and vegetables.

2. Sari gives the cashier at the music store $15 for a new CD.

3. A doctor gets paid by the government to treat sick people in a free government hospital.

4. The fisherman gives his extra fish to the leader of the tribe to give to other tribe members.

5. The farmer gives the doctor a pig in exchange for treating the farmer's sick wife.

6. This is the official mode of exchange we use in the United States.

7. The manicurist gives the teacher a manicure in exchange for the teacher tutoring the manicurist's daughter in math.

8. All the people work together to provide necessities and share everything with one another.

9. The vet treats the dentist's cat in exchange for a teeth cleaning.

10. Miguel gathers food from various farms around the village to pass out to all the community members.

CHAPTER 4

Science

> **Teachers try to change the human brain every day. The more they know about how it learns, the more successful they can be.**

The scientific technology of the last two decades has allowed teachers to know more about how students learn than any of our predecessors knew. With this information comes excitement and challenge. It is up to us to use this new knowledge to foster a love of learning in the next generation. In the field of science, this is especially true.

For a brain to store information in long-term storage areas for future recall, the learning must make sense and have meaning. Brain scans have shown that when new learning is readily comprehensible (sense) and can be connected to the past experiences (meaning), there is substantially more cerebral activity, followed by dramatically improved retention (Maquire, Frith, & Morris, 1999).

Making meaning has a tremendous impact on whether or not information will be stored. In order for students to retain the concepts they are learning, they must make a connection with their own experience. If that experience is a positive one, it is more likely students will continue to actively participate in the learning. If the experience is negative, students will likely turn off to the learning and store very little information.

Students can view science curriculum as relevant and filled with discovery or as mundane memorization. The way in which we teach makes the difference. Science is an easy subject to teach in brain-friendly ways. The curriculum lends itself to hands-on activities and discovery learning. The following activities offer brain-based strategies for teaching science standards to upper elementary students. We owe it to ourselves and our students to make science instruction meaningful and engaging. The next generation of innovation and technology depends on it.

Designed to Fit

Standards
Life Science—Understand characteristics of organisms.
Understand organisms and environments.

Objective
Students will evaluate characteristics of animals to predict their habitats and diets.

Anticipatory Set
Put on a beach hat and sunglasses, and carry a beach towel or body board. Ask students: *If I dress like this, how would you describe the environment where I live?* Give students 30 seconds to list as many adjectives as they can to describe your environment. Remove the beach attire, and put on gloves and a ski hat. Ask students: *How would you describe my environment now? List as many as you can in 30 seconds.*

Purpose
Discuss with students that your clothing provided some clues about your environment. While animals don't wear clothes, they have characteristics that make them perfectly adapted to their environments. We can make educated guesses about the habitat and diet of animals by examining some characteristics of their bodies. Tell students they are going to look at some animal parts and make predictions about where the animals live and what they eat.

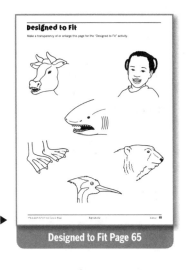

Designed to Fit Page 65

Input
Place a transparency of the **Designed to Fit reproducible (page 65)** on the overhead. Call students' attention to the pictures of a cow's teeth, a shark's teeth, and human teeth. Explain that animals' teeth are designed to help them eat different kinds of food. Ask students what they think these animals eat and what clues they used to decide.

Invite students to observe other characteristics that provide clues to an animal's habitat. Call students' attention to the other pictures on the reproducible: duck feet, furry polar bear, and woodpecker's beak. Explain that an animal's feet, skin, or fur can provide clues about where the animal lives. Guide the discussion to help students discover that animals bodies are well-suited to the environment in which they live.

Modeling

Fit for the Environment Page 66

◄ Give students a copy of the **Fit for the Environment reproducible (page 66)**. Place a transparency of the reproducible on the overhead. Point out the animal pictures. Ask students: *Based on its characteristics, what predictions can you make about the habitat and diet of each animal?*

Point out the first animal, emphasizing the webbed feet and fur. Ask students to think about what these characteristics mean and write their ideas on the page. Model for students by thinking aloud: *This animal must spend some time in water because the webbed feet would work well in water. Also, I think fur protects this animal from cold weather or cold water. I could also make a prediction about the animal's food because it does not have sharp teeth. I'll bet it's a plant eater.* Write your ideas on the transparency.

Check for Understanding

Check to make sure students understand the activity. They will look at the characteristics of each animal and make predictions about its habitat and diet.

Guided Practice

Set a timer for five minutes while students work, and play some background music (no lyrics). Circulate around the room, assisting as needed. When the timer goes off, have students take their papers and mingle around the room. When you turn off the music, have them partner with the person closest to them. Give each partner 30 seconds to defend their predictions about the first animal to their partner. Then turn on the music again, and have students find new partners. Repeat the process for all five animals.

Closure

Have students return to their seats and write the answer to the following questions in a science journal: *What can the characteristics of animals tell you about their habitat? Based on what you learned, what types of things can scientists learn about animals, such as dinosaurs, when we have only bones to study?*

Independent Practice

Have students create an imaginary creature and write a description of its habitat and diet based on its characteristics.

> **Applying new knowledge to make predictions involves higher-order thinking skills, which can increase motivation and retention.**

Designed to Fit

Make a transparency of or enlarge this page for the Designed to Fit activity.

Fit for the Environment

Directions: Use each animal's characteristics to predict its habitat and diet.

	Habitat	Diet
1. Beaver		
2. Giraffe		
3. Killer Whale		
4. Red-tailed Hawk		
5. Gray Wolf		

Reuse, Recycle, Rethink

Standard
Science in Personal and Social Perspectives—Understand populations, resources, and environments.

Objective
Students will create new uses for items normally discarded.

Anticipatory Set
Collect a garbage bag full of clean items that are normally thrown away, such as paper products, rubber bands, paper clips, straws, film canisters, soda cans, and so on. Dump out the bag on the floor at the front of the classroom. Pause and then say: *What a mess! This is just one bag of clean garbage. Can you imagine what a garbage dump must look like?*

Purpose
Inform students that each of us is partially responsible for the garbage in our environment. They are going to work together to think of ways to recycle and reuse items we normally throw away.

Input
Discuss with students that each year thousands of tons of garbage are sent to dumpsites, where it piles up for decades. As the population grows, more and more precious land resources are needed to hold all of our trash. This is already a major problem in overpopulated countries such as China and in big cities such as New York, where land is needed to house people rather than garbage. Emphasize that government leaders must develop creative ways to deal with this environmental hazard. Tell students that they are going to have the opportunity to come up with new, creative uses for trash.

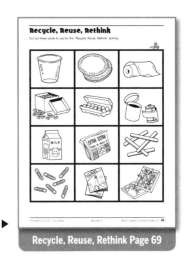

Recycle, Reuse, Rethink Page 69

Modeling
Ahead of time, copy and cut apart the cards on the **Reuse, Recycle, Rethink reproducible (page 69)**. Make two complete sets. Place each set of cards in a basket or box at the front of the room. Tell students they are going to play a game to get blood pumping to their brains and jumpstart thinking. Divide the class into two teams.

Explain the game rules: The first player on each team walks from the starting line to their team basket. The basket contains cards with the names of items we generally use once and throw away. The player takes a card from the basket, reads aloud the item written on the card, and then tells a new use for that item before returning to tag the next team member. Model how to walk (not run) to the basket, take a card, and come up with a new use for the item on the card.

Check for Understanding

Make sure students understand how to play the game. Repeat game instructions as needed, and encourage students to walk, not run.

Guided Practice

Set up the starting line and baskets with cards at the front of the room. Enforce rules about walking and voice levels as needed. Remind students that the point of the game is to hear other people's ideas about alternative uses for discarded items, so teams must remain quiet while each player speaks. Encourage creative and original ideas. Have students complete the relay race. The winning team gets first choice for the Independent Practice activity.

Independent Practice

Now that students have thought about creative uses for trash, they can put that creativity to work! Each student will choose an item from your garbage pile from the Anticipatory Set. Instruct students to determine a unique use for the item and construct that idea. For example, a plastic cup can become a question container for the teacher's desk. Ask students to write a short paragraph giving their new item a name and describing its new use.

Closure

Have students display their recycled items in a Reuse/Recycle Exhibit. Invite other classes to observe how they can recycle trash at home.

Recycle, Reuse, Rethink

Cut out these cards to use for the Recycle, Reuse, Rethink activity.

Memory Test

Standard

Science as Inquiry—Ability to conduct scientific inquiry.

Objective

Students will perform experiments to test short-term memory and learning preferences.

Anticipatory Set

Have students stand up and repeat movement patterns after you. Start easy with patterns such as: *Clap hands once, touch knees, and turn around.* Gradually add more movements to each pattern.

Purpose

Tell students they just participated in a memory test. The problem with your test, however, is that you did not record your data, so you don't have any scientific results to analyze. Explain that scientists must make sure to follow certain procedures when performing experiments so they have reliable data to answer their questions. Tell students they are going to perform experiments to obtain data and answer a question.

Input

Describe three types of learning styles people use to process new information. Auditory learners must hear something to remember it. Visual learners must see something, and tactile learners must do something. Tell students you want to find out which learning styles they like best.

Memory Test Lab Sheet Page 72

Modeling

◄ Give students a copy of the **Memory Test Lab Sheet (page 72)**. They will work with partners to perform three different experiments. Partners will do each experiment three times and use a timer to help record results. After describing each test, ask a volunteer to help you model an example for the class.

Auditory Test The first test is auditory. Student 1 is blindfolded as Student 2 prepares a simple maze for Student 1 to walk through. Student 2 gives Student 1 auditory instructions for getting through the maze. Student 2 times Student 1 as he or she completes the maze and records the time under Auditory Test on the lab sheet. Student 1 repeats

978-1-4129-5272-9

the test two more times while Student 2 records the data. Partners then reverse roles, with Student 1 giving instructions to Student 2.

Visual Test The second test is visual. Explain how to conduct the visual test. Each partner receives three copies of the visual memory test, **Visual Memory Maze (page 73)**. It's important that students not see the maze before the test begins. Student 1 times Student 2 to see how long it takes him or her to complete the maze. Student 1 records the time under Visual Test on Student 2's lab sheet. Student 2 then repeats the test two more times with Student 1 recording the times. Student 2 then gives the test to Student 1 and records the data.

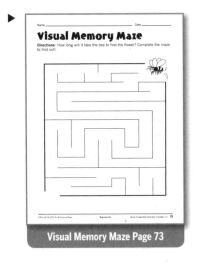

Visual Memory Maze Page 73

Tactile Test The last test is tactile. Each student uses masking tape and two stickers to create a maze on a piece of construction paper. Make sure partners don't see each other's work. Students place one sticker at the start and one sticker at the finish. Student 1 is blindfolded and must use his or her sense of touch to get through Student 2's maze from start to finish. Student 2 times Student 1 and records the data on the lab sheet. As with the other two tests, Student 1 repeats the test two more times before partners switch roles. Student 2 must then get through Student 1's maze while Student 1 times him or her.

Check for Understanding
Make sure students understand how to conduct each test prior to beginning. Explain the directions or model more examples as needed.

Guided Practice
Have student pairs complete the visual, auditory, and tactile tests as directed and record the data. Assist students as needed.

When student pairs finish all three tests, have them analyze their results. Tell students you predict that their times will be shorter on the second and third trials and that one test will show great improvement over the others.

Closure
Ask students to return to their seats and analyze their data. Ask: *Did your prediction come true?* Invite students to share on which test, or learning style, they performed best. Have them complete the bottom of the lab sheet to reflect on their experience.

Memory Test Lab Sheet

Directions : Record the data from your experiment.

Partner's Name: _____

Test 1: Auditory Test		
Trial 1 Time	Trial 2 Time	Trial 3 Time

Test 2: Visual Test		
Trial 1 Time	Trial 2 Time	Trial 3 Time

Test 3: Tactile Test		
Trial 1 Time	Trial 2 Time	Trial 3 Time

Reflections on the Experiment

When you analyze the data, which learning style (or styles) seems more natural for you?

_____

How might this information change the way you study for your next test?

_____

Visual Memory Maze

Directions: How long will it take the bee to find the flower? Complete the maze to find out!

It's a Bird! It's a Plane! It's a . . . Cloud!

Standard
Earth and Space Science—Understand changes in the earth and sky.

Objective
Students will recall and identify types of cloud formations.

Anticipatory Set
Place a piece of waxed paper and a blob of shaving cream on each student's desk. Give students 30 seconds to form a cloud shape with the shaving cream.

Purpose
Point out that each student's cloud is different, just as clouds in the sky are different. Students are going to learn about three types of clouds and identify actual examples.

> **Rehearsal helps the brain process new information.**

Input
Explain that clouds can be classified into three large groups. Scientists created these groups based on certain characteristics, such as the height and shape and how much of the sky is covered. Each group contains more detailed classification systems; however, students are going to focus on the three main types—cirrus, cumulus, and stratus. Describe cloud types to students in a demonstration with visuals, or ask students to research on their own. Lead a class discussion about cirrus, cumulus, and stratus clouds.

Cirrus clouds form very high in the sky and are thin and white with a feathery appearance. *Cumulus clouds* are cotton ball-like, puffy clouds, *Stratus clouds* are thin, layered clouds that stretch across the sky and are often gray.

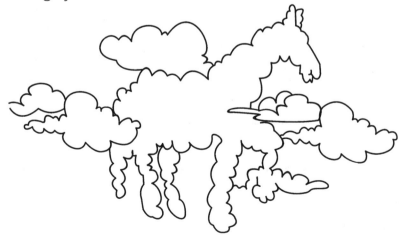

MODELING

Tell students they are now ready to go outside and identify some clouds! Before they go, they need to recall the information they just learned about clouds. Give students a copy of the **Kinds of Clouds reproducible (page 76)**. Place a transparency of the reproducible on the overhead, and point out the cloud names—cirrus, cumulus, and stratus. Demonstrate how to write a few describing words for cirrus clouds and draw a picture that reflects your description.

Guided Practice

Instruct students to write some describing words and draw a picture of each cloud type. Set a timer for five minutes, and challenge students to recall the information. Circulate around the room and assist students as needed. If students are having a hard time recalling information, prompt them with one or two descriptive adjectives.

Kinds of Clouds Page 76

Next, bring students outside to observe and sketch the clouds. If possible, take them outside to a large, grassy area where they can observe the clouds undisturbed. Tell them to use their reproducible as a guide to identify and record cloud types. Make sure each student brings the reproducible, a pencil, and something to support their reproducible while they write on it, such as a clipboard or magazine.

Closure

Return to the classroom, and ask students to share their pages with classmates. Ask them to be prepared to explain how they identified different kinds of clouds.

Extend the Activity

Discuss how people enjoy looking at clouds and finding different shapes. Ask students to share any unique shapes they've seen in clouds. Give them a copy of the **Creative Clouds reproducible (page 77)**, and point out the cloud on the page. Tell students to look at the cloud and imagine how they can transform it into something interesting or unusual. Encourage them to use markers and crayons to add details to the cloud and the background to make a picture that tells an interesting story. Allow students to transform their cloud shapes and then share their creations with the class.

Creative Clouds Page 77

Independent Practice

Have students identify different cloud types for a week. Ask them to keep a list of types and descriptions.

Kinds of Clouds

Directions: Write words or phrases to describe the clouds you saw. Then draw a picture.

Cirrus

Cumulus

Stratus

I think the clouds I saw were _____ clouds because _____

_____.

The clouds I saw looked like this:

Creative Clouds

Directions: Change the cloud into something interesting.

My cloud became a _____.

CHAPTER 5

Physical Education and the Arts

> "We have never discovered a culture on this planet—past or present—that doesn't have music, art, and dance."

Research shows that the skills involved in art activities and physical education can enhance brain function in other areas of the curriculum. Music can promote productivity and creativity in the classroom, and visual imagery can improve retention. Physical education, dance, and drama offer a multitude of opportunities for movement, which provide fuel to the brain and enhance recall. The cognitive benefits of these activities continue throughout childhood and into young adulthood. Unfortunately, art and music classes are the first to be eliminated during school budget cuts.

Music

Listening to music provides therapeutic benefits; however, there are educational benefits as well. Research studies have shown a strong correlation between music and achievement in mathematics. Music and math share several concepts: patterns, geometry, counting, ratios, proportions, equivalent fractions, and sequences. Therefore, developing the cognitive areas of the brain with music can enhance the skills needed for mathematical tasks.

Visual Arts

Imagery is visualization in the mind's eye of something a person has actually experienced. The more information an image contains, the richer and more vibrant it becomes. Students can be taught to use imagery to enhance learning and increase retention. Teachers should integrate imagery as a regular classroom strategy across the curriculum.

Movement

The more scientists study the cerebellum, the more we realize that movement and learning are inescapably linked. Physical movement increases blood flow and brings oxygen to the brain. Higher levels of oxygen in the blood significantly enhance cognitive performance. Dance, specifically, helps students become more aware of their physical presence, spatial relationships, breathing, timing, and rhythm. Engaging other cerebral aptitudes enhances integration of sensory perception.

Desert Life Mural

Objective

Students will explore textures in painting while creating a mural on desert life.

Anticipatory Set

Pretend to wipe sweat from your brow and fan yourself. Engage students by saying: *I'm thinking about a place that is very hot! I'm going to describe this place. As soon as you think you know the place I'm describing, stand up. Remember, it's hot. It gets very little rain, and it contains plants like cacti. It is home to many types of reptiles and rodents.* When you notice that most or all students are standing, invite them to say the place with you—*the desert!*

Purpose

Explain that life in the desert is full of textures. The desert is the perfect subject to explore the use of textures in painting. Tell students they are going to paint textured plants and animals for a class mural of the desert.

Input

Before beginning the activity, make sure the students have a good mental image of life in the desert Southwest of the United States. Invite them to peruse trade books, encyclopedias, and Internet sites featuring pictures of the desert. You may even ask students to research a specific plant or animal as part of a social studies or science unit. Invite them to list words to describe desert plants, animals, and objects: *The sand is grainy. Cacti are smooth with sharp thorns. Reptiles have rough, scaly skin. Rocks are craggy and bumpy.*

Modeling

Now that students have a good visual image of the desert, they can start creating a mural. On the wall, display a butcher paper background that shows a sandy desert floor and mountains in the background. See the **Desert Life Mural Example (page 81)**. Students will fill the desert with appropriate plants and animals.

> **Movement and verbalization are easy ways to stimulate thinking.**

▶ Desert Life Mural Example Page 81

Instruct students to watch as you use various objects to create different textures. Place several blobs of the same color paint on a piece of paper. Use items such as a plastic fork, a comb, and the end of a paintbrush to create unique textures in the paint. Model how different amounts of paint on a brush and varying brush strokes create different textures. Allow students to practice and explore varying techniques before proceeding with the activity.

Check for Understanding

Make sure students understand that they are responsible for creating one plant and one animal for the desert mural. These items must be native to the desert. They will employ various painting techniques to create texture.

Guided Practice

Remind students that they are each responsible for creating one plant and one animal for the desert mural. It must be a species found in the desert. They will use paint to create texture in one of two ways:

- Cover a large portion of art paper with textured paint, and then cut the plant or animal shape from the paper.

- Draw the plant or animal on art paper, and then paint it.

Allow students to spread out around the room to complete the assignment. Provide a table of art supplies, including different colored paint and a variety of texturing tools. Provide painting shirts or aprons to keep students' clothes clean. Play background music (no lyrics) with 60 beats per minute to enhance creativity and productivity. Encourage students to try various painting techniques. Instruct students to place their finished products on a drying rack when they are done. Invite them to create more items for the mural if they finish early.

Closure

Challenge students to clean their work areas and paintbrushes in the time of one well-known, upbeat song. Have them return to their seats and share answers to the following questions with a classmate: *Which item made the most interesting texture on the paint? Why did you like it? What did it look like?*

Desert Life Mural Example

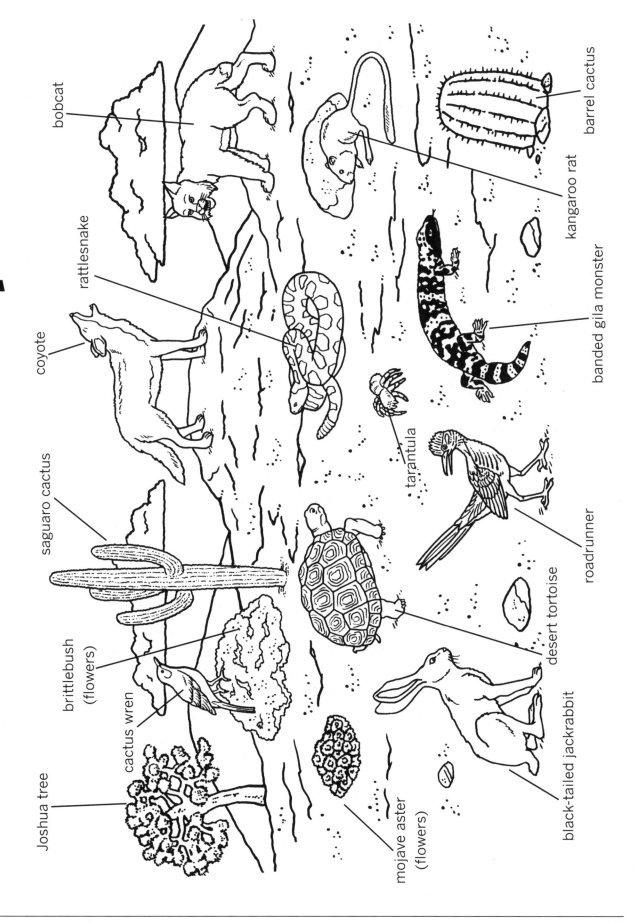

bobcat

barrel cactus

kangaroo rat

rattlesnake

coyote

banded gila monster

saguaro cactus

tarantula

roadrunner

brittlebush (flowers)

desert tortoise

Joshua tree

cactus wren

black-tailed jackrabbit

mojave aster (flowers)

Real-Life Still Life

Objective
Students will act out various inanimate objects to create a still life.

Anticipatory Set
Show examples of still-life paintings by various artists. Invite students to share their opinions and feelings about the paintings.

Purpose
Tell students they are going to be creating still-life masterpieces, but not with paint. They will use their bodies to become a real-life still life!

Input
Discuss that painters create still-life drawings and paintings by looking at a fixed arrangement and recreating it on paper. Inanimate objects are great inspiration for artists, but they are harder subjects for actors. Actors must be creative to make their bodies portray nonhuman objects. Challenge students to get their creative juices flowing as they turn their bodies into a still life.

Modeling
Invite students to practice some still lifes with you. Model for students how to act like a tree with your arms, or "branches," swaying in the wind. Model how to make your body become a bush by bending low with rounded arms.

Check for Understanding
Ask if everyone understands the objective of the activity. Remind students that you will call out an object and they will act like that object until you call out a new one.

Guided Practice
Call out objects listed on the **Real-Life Still Life samples (page 83)**. Allow students time to think before they choose a still life to interpret. Praise students for creative interpretations.

> "Movement provides novelty to a lesson and fuel to the brain."

978-1-4129-5272-9

Real-Life Still Life

Read the following directions to students for the Real-Life Still Life activity.

Turn your body into a...

- tree
- rock
- letter *Y*
- pencil
- puffy cloud
- banana
- sunflower
- starched shirt

Work with a partner or team to act out a...

- teepee
- bicycle
- letter *H*
- boat
- rocket
- book
- chair
- table
- clock showing 3:15

Closure

Encourage students to answer the following questions in a journal: *How could you use the skill we practiced today to help you in other academic subjects, such as math or spelling?*

Multicultural Moves

Objective

Students will work in cooperative groups to write a fictional story and create a dance that tells the story.

Anticipatory Set

Lead students in singing a song with motions such as "The Wheels on the Bus" or "The Itsy Bitsy Spider."

Purpose

Tell students they are going to write a story and then create a dance to help tell it.

Input

Tell students that cultures throughout history have used some form of dance and that many use dance to tell stories. The Hawaiian hula is an example of a dance used to tell stories. Dancers use their hands and body movements to communicate. Show a video of dancers doing the hula, or use the Internet to find short video clips.

Students will use two forms of communication to tell a story. First, they will write a fictitious tale, and then they will create hand motions and a dance to share their tale with the class.

PART 1

Modeling

The first step in the lesson is writing a story. Divide the class into teams, and give each team one **Team Tale reproducible (page 86)**. Teams will create a story one sentence at a time. Student 1 completes the first sentence by making up an ending to the prompt. Student 1 then passes the page to the student on his or her right. Student 2 reads the first sentence and makes up a second sentence.

Model these steps with one of the teams. Explain that teammates keep taking turns until they finish their story. Continue modeling until students have a good grasp of the concept.

Team Tale Page 86

Check for Understanding

Model the process again as needed. Students generally catch on easily once they see this activity modeled.

Guided Practice

Watch carefully as teams begin writing their stories. If you are concerned teammates won't follow the process, have each team member use a different colored writing instrument for individual accountability. Circulate around the room and assist as needed. Set a timer for 10 to 15 minutes, depending on the desired story length. Give a signal when time is almost up so students can conclude their stories.

PART 2

Modeling

Remind students that the second part of the lesson is to create a dance (body and hand movements) that tells their story. They may select one student to read the story aloud as the rest of the team performs the dance. Demonstrate how to tell a story through dance. Use a well-known nursery rhyme as an example.

Check for Understanding

Make sure students understand the activity before beginning. Remind them that all team members must participate either by reading or by dancing.

Guided Practice

Allow teams to spread out in the classroom to work on and rehearse their dances. Suggest that students brainstorm ideas and then come to a team consensus on how each movement will tell a part of the story. Assist students as needed. Praise teams for creative ideas and for working well together.

After ample practice time, invite teams to perform their dances for the class. Videotape performances so students can watch and compare all the dances.

Closure

Ask students to share which dances told the best stories and why. Then prompt students to write about their experiences by completing the **Reflections on Team Tale reproducible (page 87)**.

Reflections on Team Tale Page 87

Name ______________________________ Date ______________

Team Tale

Directions: Create a story. Each team member must contribute.

Team Members: ______________________ ______________________

______________________ ______________________

______________________ ______________________

Once upon a time in a village far, far away...

 978-1-4129-5272-9 • *© Corwin Press*

Reflections on Team Tale

Directions: Write your thoughts about the activity in the spaces below.

Team Members: _____ _____

_____ _____

_____ _____

Basic story plot:

| |
| |

The best part of our story was:	The best part of our dance was:

Our team worked well together when:	We could have done better by:

I am a good team member when I:	I could be a better teammate by:

The Color of Music

Objective

Students will interpret the emotional effect of music through the use of color.

Anticipatory Set

Play age-appropriate blues music for students. Inform students that this music is called *the blues*. Ask: *How do you think it earned that name?* Allow students to share their responses with a classmate, and then invite them to share their ideas.

Purpose

Explain that all music produces some kind of emotion in people, just as colors make people feel different ways. Tell students they are going to use color to show how various types of music make them feel.

Input

Discuss that if someone says he or she has "the blues," we generally assume the person is sad. Blues music is also usually sad. The color blue is often associated with sadness, but it may also make us feel peaceful. Colors can make people feel different emotions. There are no right or wrong answers to how colors or music make people feel. In this activity, students will explore feelings that music and colors evoke.

Modeling

Tell students that you are going to play several different types of music. They will listen to the music and visualize colors or pictures that represent the music. Students then use those colors to create a work of art. It can be an abstract use of colors or realistic pictures visualized when listening to the music.

Get a piece of art paper and crayons or oil pastels. Play a piece of music such as "Spring" from Vivaldi's *Four Seasons* to inspire imagination and creativity. Prompt students to close their eyes and listen carefully. Ask students: *What emotions do you feel when you listen to this music? Are there any colors or pictures that come to mind when you hear it? I'm going to use colors and pictures to express how the music makes me feel.*

Draw a picture as the music plays. After a short period of time, stop the music, and display what you've drawn so far. Explain why you chose particular colors and pictures. Describe how the music made you feel and how you tried to express it with colors.

> **Visualization is a skill that aids in retention and is necessary for survival.**

978-1-4129-5272-9

Check for Understanding

Make sure everyone understands how to proceed with the activity. Some students may have difficulty expressing abstract ideas such as feelings from music. Assure students that there are no right or wrong answers. Art is a personal expression of what we see in our minds.

Guided Practice

Give students a piece of art paper and crayons or oil pastels. Have them fold their paper to form four equal sections. Explain to students: *I am going to play four different pieces of music. You will listen to the music and create a piece of art that shows how it makes you feel or what you see in your mind.*

Choose four different pieces of music. Classical music works well, but you can also experiment with other types of music. Try to stay away from music that is very familiar to students or that has words. Have students write the name of each music piece in the lower left corner of a section of their paper. Play the music one piece at a time. Invite students to imitate what you modeled, expressing their thoughts, feelings, and ideas using different colors and pictures. When they are finished, students will have one piece of paper with four different visual interpretations of the music.

While they are drawing, students may ask what you think about the music. Try to refrain from giving your own interpretations, and encourage students to think and draw freely.

Closure

Display students' artwork around the classroom. Invite volunteers to share their interpretations of the music, including color and picture choices. Urge them to describe how the music made them feel. To close, have students complete the **My Colors of Music reproducible (page 90)** to reflect on their experiences.

My Colors of Music Page 90

My Colors of Music

Directions: Write about how different kinds of music make you feel.

1. My favorite piece of music was _____.

2. I liked this music because it made me feel _____
_____.

3. It reminded me of the color (or colors) _____.

4. I drew a picture of _____ to go with
my favorite piece of music.

5. The piece of music I liked least was _____
_____.

6. This music made me feel _____
_____.

7. I chose to represent that piece by drawing _____.

8. This music reminded me of the color (or colors) _____.

9. My favorite kind of music is _____ because it makes me feel
_____.

Sequential Movement

Objective

Students will work as a group to create a movement sequence.

Anticipatory Set

Stand at the front of the class. When you have everyone's attention, perform a series of movements. Pause between each move to emphasize the distinct order—beginning, middle, and end. Your routine may look something like a move in martial arts or a cheerleading routine.

Purpose

Tell students they are going to work with a group to create a sequence of movements and demonstrate it for the class.

Input

Discuss with students the distinct steps in a movement. For example, demonstrate the basic movements involved in the swing of a golf club or tennis racquet or the fielding of a softball. Emphasize the importance of breaking down the sequence of the movement to learn and understand the correct procedure. Consider showing a videotape in slow motion to identify distinct movements.

Modeling

Make a transparency of the **Sequential Movement reproducible (page 93)**. Show students how to complete the flowchart. In each box, write a sentence to describe the movement, and draw an accompanying illustration. Demonstrate each distinct motion, and then combine them into a fluid movement.

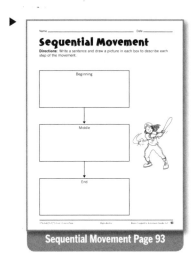

Sequential Movement Page 93

Check for Understanding

Use a quick assessment technique to check for understanding. Try "thumbs up" for understanding and "thumbs down" for more explanation. Describe the activity again if students are unsure how to proceed, or complete another transparency of the reproducible from start to finish.

Guided Practice

Ask students to form groups of three. Tell them to break down the motions involved in a chosen movement into a three-part sequence.

They can use this sequence to teach the movement to classmates. Encourage group members try out each motion before recording the steps on the Sequential Movement flowchart. Urge them to make sure their instructions (or steps) are written clearly and concisely in the correct order.

Closure

Have each group demonstrate the sequences they created. Encourage them to explain each step as they demonstrate. Prompt other students to ask questions or volunteer to follow instructions to repeat the movements.

Independent Practice

Have students reflect on the activity in their journals. Ask them to respond to the following questions: *What was the most valuable thing I learned from this activity? How is it useful to break down the steps into a logical sequence?*

Sequential Movement

Directions: Write a sentence and draw a picture in each box to describe each step of the movement.

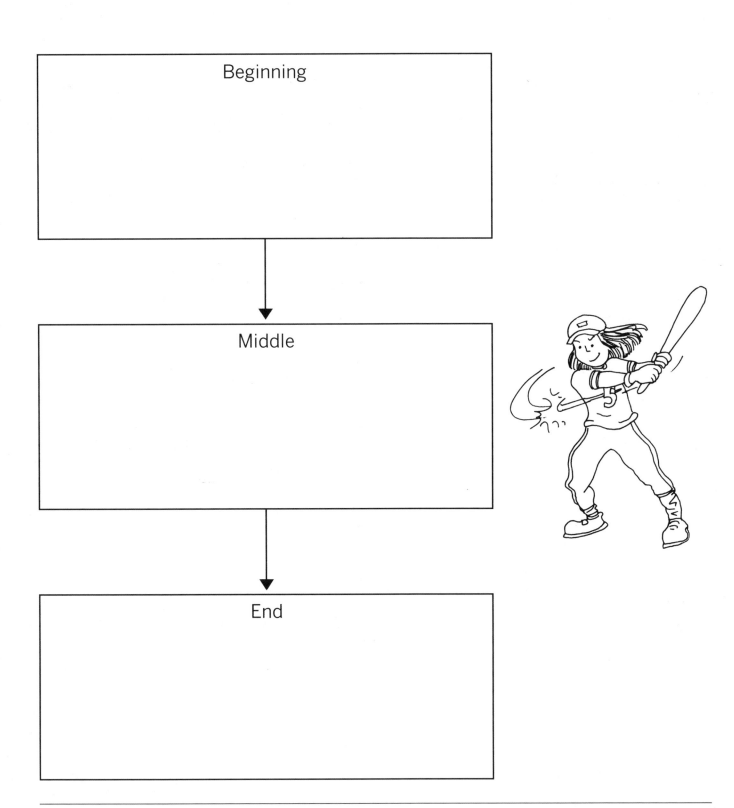

Beginning

Middle

End

Answer Key

FORMAL OR INFORMAL (PAGE 15)

1. informal
2. formal
3. informal
4. informal
5. formal
6. informal
7. formal
8. informal
9. formal
10. informal
11. formal
12. informal

SHOW ME Y! (PAGE 30)

1. 4
2. 5
3. 9
4. 3
5. 8
6. 16
7. 8
8. 7
9. 42
10. 4

Answers to questions will vary.

GIVE ME A Y! (PAGE 31)

1. 5
2. 12
3. 56
4. 21
5. 9
6. 8
7. 3
8. 4
9. 11
10. 36

Answers will vary.

PATTERN BLOCK DESIGN (PAGE 34)

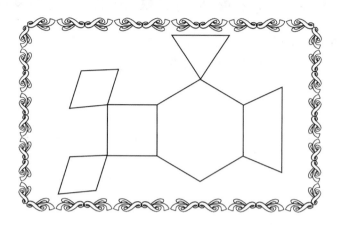

FIND THE ACORN 2 (PAGE 42)

1. 3
2. –1
3. –7
4. –5
5. 0
6. 4
7. 10
8. 2
9. –2
10. –8
11. 8
12. –4

SURFING THE NUMBER LINE (PAGE 43)

1. 6
2. –7
3. –1
4. 2
5. –10
6. –5
7. 2
8. 2, –2
9. –2, –5
10. –5, 3
11. 3, 8
12. 8, 0

978-1-4129-5272-9

TRANSCONTINENTAL RAILROAD (PAGE 53)

Who? Central Pacific Railroad and Union Pacific Railroad **What?** Central Pacific Railroad and Union Pacific Railroad connected to form the first transcontinental railroad in the United States. It ran 3,500 miles from New York to California. **When?** May 10, 1869 **Where?** Promontory Summit, Utah **Why?** So passengers could travel from the east to the west coast of the United States in only six days **How?** Both companies worked several years and used thousands of workers to complete the task.

TERMS OF TRADE (PAGE 61)

1. reciprocity
2. money
3. redistribution
4. redistribution
5. barter
6. money
7. barter
8. reciprocity
9. barter
10. redistribution

FIT FOR THE ENVIRONMENT (PAGE 66)

1. Beaver habitat: semi-aquatic environment (webbed hind feet with clawed toes for digging); rich, thick fur (waterproof and insulating), paddle-shaped hairless tail. Lives in rivers, streams, lakes, ponds, swamps, and other wetland areas.
   Beaver diet: Herbivore, eats leaves, shoots, twigs, roots, bark, weeds, and grasses (large front teeth, with short, flat back teeth)
2. Giraffe habitat: Dry, open wooded areas in the savanna (short hair with spots for camouflage from enemies; long neck to see above trees)
   Giraffe diet: herbivore; eats mainly leaves and buds of acacia trees (flat teeth; long tongue; long neck to reach high)
3. Killer whale habitat: All oceans of the world, mostly the Arctic and Antarctic (fins and blubber for warmth)
   Killer whale diet: Carnivore, eats penguins, birds, otters, fish, squid, sea lions, sea turtles, (lots of long, sharp teeth)
4. Red-tailed hawk habitat: Spends a lot of time in the air (large wings and feathers; large, sharp eyes) in the open country of North America, Canada, and Alaska
   Red-tailed hawk diet: Carnivore, eats small mammals, mice, rats, moles, shrews, squirrels, muskrats, birds (large, hooked beak; sharp talons on feet)
5. Gray wolf habitat: Cold, forested areas of Northern Michigan, Minnesota, and Wisconsin (long, thick fur)
   Gray wolf diet: Carnivore, eats anything from field mice to huge caribou (long, sharp teeth)

VISUAL MEMORY TEST (PAGE 73)

References

Gurian, M., & Henley, P. (2001). *Boys and girls learn differently!* San Francisco, CA: Jossey-Bass.

Kagan, S. (1994). *Cooperative learning.* San Clemente, CA: Kagan Publishing.

Kagan, S. (2000). *Silly sports and goofy games.* San Clemente, CA: Kagan Publishing.

Kathee, T. (1997). *Observing clouds.* Retrieved July 19, 2006, from http://vathena.arc.nasa.gov.

A Lifetime of Color™. (n.d.). *Into the spectacular sea.* Retrieved July 17, 2006, from http://www.sanford-artedventures.com.

A Lifetime of Color™. (n.d.). *Music and color.* Retrieved July 17, 2006, from http://www.sanford-artedventures.com.

Maquire, E. A., Frith, C. D., & Morris, R. G. M. (1999). The functional neuroanatomy of comprehension and memory: The importance of prior knowledge. *Brain, 122,* 1,839–1,850.

National Council for the Social Studies. (2002). *Expectations of excellence: Curriculum standards for social studies.* Silver Spring, MD: National Council for the Social Studies (NCSS).

National Council of Teachers of English and International Reading Association. (1996). *Standards for the English language arts.* Urbana, IL: National Council of Teachers of English (NCTE).

National Council of Teachers of Mathematics. (2005). *Principles and standards for school mathematics.* Reston, VA: National Council of Teachers of Mathematics (NCTM).

National Research Council. (2005). *National science education standards.* Washington, DC: National Academy Press.

San Filippo, M. (n.d.). *Buon natale! Christmas in Italy.* Retrieved July 5, 2006, from http://www.about.com.

Smith, D. (n.d.). *The transcontinental railroad.* Retrieved July 6, 2006, from http://www.about.com.

Sousa, D. A. (2006). *How the brain learns, 3rd edition.* Thousand Oaks, CA: Corwin Press.

Stark, R. (2001). *Anthropology: Teacher edition.* Hawthorne, NJ: Educational Impressions, Inc.